COOKING WITH
Bon Appétit

COOKING WITH
Bon Appétit

One-Dish Meals

THE KNAPP PRESS
Publishers
Los Angeles

Copyright © 1985 by Knapp Communications Corporation

Published by The Knapp Press
5900 Wilshire Boulevard, Los Angeles, California 90036

Library of Congress Cataloging in Publication Data

Main entry under title:

One-dish meals.

  (Cooking with Bon appétit)
  Includes index.
  1. Casserole cookery. 2. Cookery (Entrées)
I. Series.
TX693.045 1986   641.8'21   85-24004
ISBN 0-89535-171-4

On the cover: *Vosges Mountain Sausage and Vegetable Pot*

Printed and bound in the United States of America

10   9   8   7   6   5   4   3   2   1

❧ Contents

🍎 Foreword

For ease of preparation and simplicity in serving, one-dish meals are a cook's dream come true. When a menu features multiple courses, there is always the challenge of having everything ready at the right moment—sometimes a trickier feat than it seems, even if the dishes themselves are uncomplicated. The solution? A meal in a dish (or tureen or skillet), requiring nothing more than a loaf of crusty bread, a tossed salad or a bowl of steamed rice to round it out.

To some people, "one-dish meal" calls up childhood memories of bland tuna casseroles and endless variations on ground beef. This collection of nearly 200 *Bon Appétit* recipes will banish those associations forever. Naturally there are casseroles here—but such selections as Swiss-style Scalloped Onions and Ham (page 108), Northern-style Chinese One-Pot (page 100), and Luxurious Crab and Artichoke Casserole (page 68) are anything but ordinary.

And a casserole is only one among many choices. Nearly every category of food offers an ample selection of one-dish meals: hearty soups and stews, rice and pasta specialties, savory pies and quiches, braises and stir-fries, omelets, main-dish salads. Some are quick and simple enough for a weekday supper for the family. Others, definitely party fare, include such spectaculars as Turkey Breast Wellington (page 25), a classic Bollito Misto (page 95), and zesty Fisherman's Stew (page 74), boasting seven varieties of seafood.

In short, there is always a one-dish meal to fit the bill—whether you want to entertain elegantly or to keep the occasion casual. Our selection of *Bon Appétit's* best will show you the possibilities.

1 ❧ Soups

We must make a concession here: The soups in this chapter are not, strictly speaking, one-dish meals. They are, more accurately, one-*bowl* meals—and wonderfully robust and satisfying ones at that.

These hearty soups star in country kitchens all over the world. The West Indies boasts an unusual one called Callaloo (page 2), traditionally made with taro leaves; our version uses spinach, more readily available and equally tasty. Colombia's *Ajiaco Bogotano* (page 10), a lavish chicken and potato mixture garnished with sour cream, corn, avocados and capers, is considered so special that it is generally reserved for holiday gatherings. Also potato-based but entirely different is Portuguese Green Soup (page 13), often accompanied by the whole wheat corn bread called *broa*. And then there are opulent seafood chowders, as well as lusty soup-stews typical of various European regions: Split Pea One-Pot (page 5) from Germany, Tuscan White Bean and Tomato Soup (page 6), and Belgium's classic *Potée d'Ardennes* (page 11).

You might not plan a formal dinner party around these dishes, but you won't find anything better for casual entertaining. The soups are rustic, warming, the very soul of "comfort food"—and the perfect choice when family and friends gather for good company and good eating.

Cabbage Soup with Roquefort Cheese

8 to 12 servings

1 meaty ham bone
¼ cup (½ stick) butter
2 large onions, chopped
1 bunch celery, chopped
2 leeks, chopped
1½ quarts chicken stock or
    light veal stock
1½ quarts water
1 2½-pound cabbage, cored and
    cut into small wedges
1 pound carrots, peeled and cut
    into 1-inch pieces
1 pound turnips, peeled and cut
    into 1-inch pieces
1 pound potatoes, peeled and cut
    into 1-inch pieces

⅔ cup large dried white beans,
    soaked overnight in water
    to cover
2 turnips, chopped
2 carrots, chopped
4 garlic cloves, minced
    Bouquet garni (2 parsley sprigs,
    1 fresh thyme sprig or
    ¼ teaspoon dried, crumbled, and
    1 bay leaf)

Salt and freshly ground pepper
8 to 12 slices whole wheat bread,
    crusts trimmed, lightly toasted
    and halved
    Roquefort cheese, crumbled

Remove meat from ham bone; reserve bone. Cut meat into small pieces. Melt butter in heavy Dutch oven over low heat. Add ham, onions, celery and leeks. Cook until vegetables are soft, stirring occasionally, about 20 minutes. Add stock, water and ham bone and bring to boil. Add cabbage. Reduce heat and simmer 30 minutes. Add 1 pound carrots, 1 pound turnips and potatoes. Simmer 1 hour.

Meanwhile, drain beans. Transfer to heavy medium saucepan. Pour in enough water to cover by 1½ inches. Add 2 turnips, 2 carrots, garlic and bouquet garni. Simmer until beans are tender, about 1½ hours.

Drain beans, discarding bouquet garni. Add beans to soup and bring to boil. Season with salt and pepper. Just before serving, place 2 toast halves in each soup bowl. Top with crumbled cheese. Ladle soup over cheese.

Callaloo

Authentic West Indian callaloo is difficult to make in the United States because callaloo (taro) leaves are unavailable and fresh coconuts a rarity in many parts of the country. This recipe produces a good approximation of the original using frozen chopped spinach and "milk" made from canned flaked coconut.

6 to 8 servings

3 tablespoons bacon fat or
    ham drippings
1 large yellow onion, chopped
1 large garlic clove, minced
½ medium-size green bell pepper,
    cored, seeded and chopped

2 cups boiling water
1 3½-ounce can flaked coconut

1 10-ounce package frozen
    chopped spinach, thawed
½ 10-ounce package frozen cut
    okra, thawed
1 large boiling potato (about
    8 ounces), peeled and cut into
    ½-inch cubes

1 medium-size sweet potato or yam
    (about 8 ounces), peeled and cut
    into ½-inch cubes
2½ cups (or more) beef stock
1 tablespoon snipped fresh chives
¼ teaspoon dried thyme, crumbled
¼ teaspoon freshly grated nutmeg
½ cup chopped dried beef
⅛ to ¼ teaspoon cayenne pepper
    Salt and freshly ground pepper

Melt bacon fat or drippings in heavy 6-quart saucepan over medium-high heat. Add onion, garlic and green pepper and sauté until limp and lightly browned, about 10 to 15 minutes.

Meanwhile, combine boiling water and coconut in bowl and steep 10 minutes. Transfer water and coconut to processor or blender and mix 2 minutes (use high speed with blender). Pour coconut mixture into fine sieve set over bowl. Using wooden spoon, press out as much "milk" as possible. Reserve liquid (you should have about 1¾ cups); discard solids.

Add spinach and okra to saucepan and sauté 5 minutes. Stir in coconut milk, potatoes, 2½ cups stock, chives, thyme and nutmeg. Reduce heat to very low, cover and simmer until mixture is consistency of thick vegetable soup, stirring occasionally, about 3 hours. Transfer ¾ (about 6 cups) of soup mixture to food processor or blender in batches and puree (or pass mixture through fine disc of food mill). Return pureed mixture to saucepan. Stir in dried beef, cayenne, salt and pepper to taste. Cover and simmer over very low heat 30 minutes. Taste and add more salt if desired. Soup can be thinned with additional beef stock; it should have consistency of thick vegetable cream soup.

Parsnip Stew

A cross between an early New England chowder and stew that features a variety of winter vegetables. Serve with freshly baked biscuits.

4 to 6 servings

12 ounces lean salt pork, cut into small cubes
2 medium carrots, diced
1 large onion, finely chopped
3 large or 5 small parsnips, peeled, cored if necessary and diced
1 cup tightly packed chopped green cabbage

1 medium potato, peeled and diced
5 cups rich chicken stock
1 bay leaf
Pinch of ground cloves
Generous pinch of dried thyme or ¼ teaspoon minced fresh
Salt and freshly ground pepper

Blanch salt pork by dropping into boiling water for 5 minutes. Drain well and rinse. Sauté salt pork in heavy 4- to 5-quart saucepan over medium heat until golden. Remove with slotted spoon and set aside. Pour off all but about 2 tablespoons fat from pan. Add carrot and onion and sauté until onion is soft. Add salt pork and remaining ingredients and bring to simmer. Cook uncovered until vegetables are tender but still have slight crunch, about 10 minutes. Serve hot.

Stew can be prepared several days before serving and refrigerated, or frozen in airtight container up to 3 months.

Winter Vegetable Soup with Dill

Serve with slices of whole-grain bread for a satisfying family dinner.

6 servings

2½ tablespoons butter
2 medium leeks, trimmed and coarsely chopped (about 4 cups)
2 medium kohlrabi, trimmed, peeled and coarsely diced (about 4 cups; chop and reserve any small tender leaves)
1 small turnip, well trimmed, peeled and coarsely diced (about ¾ cup)
2½ tablespoons all purpose flour
5 cups rich chicken stock, preferably homemade
¼ cup chopped fresh dill or

2 tablespoons dried dillweed
¾ teaspoon salt
⅛ teaspoon freshly ground pepper

1 medium potato, peeled and diced (about 1¼ cups)
⅔ cup sour cream, room temperature
Fresh dill sprigs
Additional sour cream

Melt butter in 3-quart saucepan over medium-high heat. Add leeks and sauté just until limp, 4 to 5 minutes; *do not brown*. Add kohlrabi and turnip, reduce heat to medium-low and cook 1 minute, stirring constantly. Sprinkle flour over vegetables and mix thoroughly. Gradually blend in chicken stock. Stir in chopped dill, salt and pepper. Cover and simmer 12 minutes.

Add potato to soup. Cover and simmer until vegetables are tender, 10 to 12 minutes. (*Soup can be prepared 1 day ahead to this point and refrigerated. Reheat before continuing.*) Combine sour cream with about ½ cup soup broth in small bowl and blend until smooth. Gradually add sour cream mixture back to soup, stirring constantly; *do not let soup return to boil*. Season with salt if desired. Ladle soup into heated bowls. Garnish with dill and sour cream and serve.

Walter's Legendary Lentil Soup

A comforting soup for cold weather.

6 to 8 servings

1 tablespoon unsalted butter
6 ounces smoked ham, cut into ¼-inch cubes (1 generous cup)
8 to 10 cups beef stock
1 pound lentils
1 small dried red chili
  Pinch of dried savory, crumbled

¼ cup olive oil
2 medium onions, chopped
2 medium carrots, peeled and diced
1 medium-size red bell pepper, diced

2 large garlic cloves, minced

3 tablespoons unsalted butter
3 tablespoons all purpose flour
1 cup tomato puree
4 tablespoons balsamic or red wine vinegar
  Salt and freshly ground pepper
  Sautéed Croutons*

Melt 1 tablespoon butter in heavy Dutch oven over medium heat. Add ham and cook 5 minutes, stirring occasionally. Add 6 cups stock, lentils, chili and savory. Cover and bring to boil. Reduce heat and simmer until lentils are tender but firm to bite, stirring occasionally, about 30 minutes.

Heat oil in heavy large skillet over medium heat. Add onions, carrots and bell pepper. Stir until vegetables begin to soften, about 5 minutes. Add garlic and cook 2 minutes. Stir mixture into soup. Add enough stock to cover.

Wipe out skillet. Add 3 tablespoons butter and melt over medium-low heat. Add flour and stir until light brown, about 6 minutes. Whisk in 2 cups stock. Bring to boil, whisking constantly. Add to soup. Stir in tomato puree and 3 tablespoons vinegar. Bring to boil. Reduce heat, cover and simmer 30 minutes, skimming surface and stirring occasionally. Thin soup to desired consistency with stock. Season with remaining 1 tablespoon vinegar, salt and generous amount of pepper. Discard chili. Garnish soup with croutons and serve.

*Sautéed Croutons

Makes about 2 cups

¼ cup (½ stick) butter
¼ cup olive oil

½ loaf white bread (crusts trimmed), cubed

Melt butter with oil in heavy large skillet over medium heat. Add bread cubes and stir gently until golden brown. Drain on paper towels.

Split Pea One-Pot (Erbsen Eintopf)

4 to 5 servings

3 tablespoons butter
2 large onions, diced
¼ cup chopped fresh parsley
3 tablespoons finely diced celery root or celery (with leaves)
2 medium-size russet potatoes, peeled and finely diced
6 cups water
2 cups quick-cooking split peas, rinsed and drained
2 bay leaves, bruised
½ teaspoon freshly ground pepper
Generous pinch of ground cloves

1½ cups finely diced smoked ham (preferably country ham)
⅔ cup dry German white wine

4 to 5 strips bacon (preferably country cured), coarsely diced
1 large onion, sliced into ⅛-inch rings

Chicken stock (optional)
⅓ cup sour cream
Salt

Melt butter in stockpot or large Dutch oven over medium-high heat. Add onion, parsley and celery root and cook, stirring constantly, until limp. Stir in potatoes, water, peas, bay leaves, pepper and cloves and bring to boil. Reduce heat to low, cover and simmer, stirring occasionally, about 1 hour.

Add ham and wine. Cover and cook, stirring occasionally, until peas are tender, adding more water if necessary to prevent sticking, about 1 hour.

Meanwhile, cook bacon in heavy medium skillet over high heat until almost crisp. Remove with slotted spoon and drain on paper towels. Discard all but 2 tablespoons fat from skillet. Reduce heat to medium, add onion rings and cook, stirring frequently, until golden. Drain on paper towels.

Stir chicken stock into split pea mixture if thinner consistency is desired and cook until heated through. Stir in sour cream. Remove from heat. Discard bay leaves and season with salt.

Divide among heated individual soup plates or bowls. Top each with bacon and onion rings and serve.

Ribollita (Twice-cooked Bean Soup)

A ribsticking Italian soup-stew.

6 to 8 servings

8 ounces dried white beans (1½ cups)

1 ham hock or prosciutto bone

¼ cup olive oil
½ cup chopped onion
1 medium leek, trimmed and chopped
1 medium carrot, chopped
1 medium celery stalk, chopped
½ medium head red cabbage, shredded, or 4 cups shredded Savoy cabbage
1 small bunch kale (if available), shredded
1 unpeeled potato, cut into chunks (1 cup)

1 small bunch Swiss chard, shredded (3 cups)
1 large tomato or 1 cup canned tomatoes, chopped
2 garlic cloves, minced
1½ teaspoons dried rosemary, crumbled
1½ teaspoons chopped fresh parsley
½ teaspoon dried thyme, crumbled
Salt and freshly ground pepper

6 ½- to ¾-inch-thick slices Italian or French bread, toasted
1 cup freshly grated Parmesan cheese (5 ounces)
½ cup thinly sliced onion
½ cup olive oil (optional)

Combine beans in large saucepan with enough cold water to cover. Let stand at room temperature overnight.

Drain beans well; return to saucepan. Add ham hock and enough water to cover generously. Bring to boil over high heat. Reduce heat to medium-low and simmer until beans are tender, about 1½ hours. Drain, reserving liquid and ham hock. Transfer half of beans to processor or blender and puree (or put through strainer); reserve whole beans. Discard ham bone; cut meat into small pieces.

Heat ¼ cup olive oil in Dutch oven or large saucepan over medium-high heat. Add chopped onion, leek, carrot and celery and sauté until softened, about 5 minutes. Blend in cabbage, kale, potato, pureed beans and about 6 cups reserved bean cooking liquid, adding water if necessary to make 6 cups. Bring to simmer over medium-high heat, then reduce heat to medium and simmer until all vegetables are tender, about 30 minutes.

Add Swiss chard, tomato, garlic, rosemary, parsley, thyme, salt, pepper and reserved ham. Simmer until chard is tender and flavors are well blended, at least 1 hour, adding more bean cooking liquid or water if soup is too thick.

Stir in whole beans and simmer until heated through, 5 to 10 minutes. Cool; cover and refrigerate overnight.

Preheat oven to 375°F. Arrange toast in bottom of ovenproof soup tureen. Sprinkle with ½ cup Parmesan cheese. Bring soup to boil. Ladle soup over toast. Top with sliced onion, remaining ½ cup cheese and ½ cup olive oil if desired. Bake until bubbling, about 25 to 30 minutes. Serve immediately.

Some of soup can be served without bread and remainder "reboiled" with toast the following day for ribollita. Reduce amount of bread or add more reserved bean cooking liquid or water if soup is too thick.

Tuscan White Bean and Tomato Soup

For a perfect summer supper, serve this hearty country soup with crusty bread and a tossed green salad.

Makes 4 quarts

1 pound dried Great Northern beans

4 cups chicken stock, preferably homemade
2 bay leaves

⅓ cup olive oil
12 ounces onions, thinly sliced
4 medium celery stalks, thinly sliced
3 medium carrots, thinly sliced
5 to 6 ounces pancetta,* cut into ¼-inch cubes

10 ounces smoked ham, coarsely diced
2 teaspoons sugar
4 garlic cloves, minced
5 pounds (about 12 large) ripe tomatoes, peeled, seeded and coarsely chopped

¼ cup fresh lemon juice
Salt and freshly ground pepper
Minced fresh parsley

Soak beans in cold water to cover in stockpot overnight. (Or boil beans 3 minutes, then soak 1 hour.)

Add stock and bay leaves to beans. Simmer until tender, about 1 hour.

Heat oil in heavy large saucepan over medium-high heat. Add onions, celery and carrots and stir until softened and just beginning to color, about 5 minutes. Add pancetta and stir until translucent, about 3 minutes. Add ham, sugar and garlic and stir 5 minutes. Stir in tomatoes and bring to boil. Reduce heat to simmer. Add beans and liquid and cook until thick, stirring occasionally, about 45 minutes.

Blend in lemon juice. Season with salt and pepper. Let soup stand at room temperature several hours. Sprinkle with parsley before serving.

*Italian-style unsmoked bacon, preserved in salt. Available at Italian markets.

Aunt Laura's Fish Chowder

8 servings

2 tablespoons (¼ stick) butter
1 medium onion, chopped
¼ cup all purpose flour
5 cups milk

2 tablespoons salt
1 pound haddock or scrod fillets
3 carrots, diced

1 large potato, peeled and diced
1 10-ounce package frozen
   peas, thawed
Salt and freshly ground pepper

Melt butter in 1½-quart saucepan over low heat. Add onion and cook until tender, about 10 minutes. Blend in flour, stirring constantly until mixture is smooth. Continue to cook, stirring frequently, until thickened, about 3 minutes. Gradually add milk, stirring constantly until well blended. Remove from heat and set aside.

    Bring 2 quarts water to boil with salt in 4-quart saucepan over medium-high heat. Add fish; return water to boil. Reduce heat and simmer until barely tender, about 10 minutes. Transfer fish to platter using slotted spoon and set aside. Pour off half of fish poaching liquid. Add carrot to pan and boil 5 minutes. Add potato and cook over medium-high heat until vegetables are tender, about 15 minutes. Blend in peas and cook 2 to 3 minutes. Add milk mixture and blend thoroughly. Slice fish into several pieces and return to saucepan. Continue cooking until chowder is heated through. Season with salt and pepper. Ladle into bowls and serve immediately.

Lee's Lobster Pot Soup

8 servings

3 tablespoons butter
2 onions, thinly sliced
1 garlic clove, chopped
2 quarts (or more) beef stock
1 8-ounce package small
   shell macaroni
1 1-pound can whole tomatoes,
   chopped (reserve liquid)
1 large bunch spinach, coarsely
   chopped, or one 10-ounce
   package frozen chopped spinach,
   thawed

1 8- to 10-ounce package frozen
   lobster tails, thawed and chopped
1 bay leaf
½ teaspoon dried basil, crumbled
   Cayenne pepper

Melt butter in heavy large saucepan over medium-high heat. Add onion and garlic, cover and cook until onion is translucent, about 7 minutes. Pour in 2 quarts stock and bring to boil. Add macaroni and cook 5 minutes, stirring frequently. Stir in tomatoes and liquid, spinach, lobster, bay leaf, basil and cayenne. Cover and simmer until macaroni is tender, about 8 minutes. Add more broth if thinner consistency is desired. Ladle into bowls and serve hot.

Brazilian Mussel Chowder

8 servings

36 mussels, scrubbed and debearded
2 cups dry white wine
1 medium leek, chopped
½ cup chopped fresh parsley

6 cups whipping cream
1½ cups flaked coconut

¼ cup (½ stick) butter
1 medium onion, finely chopped
2 cups fresh corn kernels
1 jalapeño pepper, roasted, peeled and minced

1 parsley sprig
1 cilantro sprig
2 tablespoons grated fresh ginger
Salt and freshly ground pepper
1 cup fresh corn kernels, blanched
1 cup diced zucchini, blanched
1 cup diced carrot, blanched
1 medium-size red bell pepper, roasted, peeled, seeded and diced
¼ cup cilantro leaves

Combine mussels, wine, leek and chopped parsley in heavy large pot over high heat. Cover and cook until mussels open, shaking pan occasionally, about 4 minutes. Remove opened mussels. Cook unopened mussels 3 more minutes. Discard remaining unopened mussels. Strain liquid into small saucepan, using sieve lined with several layers of dampened cheesecloth. Boil liquid until reduced by almost ⅓. Remove mussels from shells.

Meanwhile, boil cream with coconut in large saucepan until reduced by half. Stir in mussel liquid.

Melt butter in heavy large saucepan over medium-low heat. Add onion and cook until translucent, stirring occasionally, about 10 minutes. Add 2 cups corn, jalapeño, parsley and cilantro sprigs and cook until softened, stirring occasionally, about 5 minutes. Stir in cream mixture and ginger and heat through. Puree in blender. Strain back into saucepan. Rewarm soup gently. Season with salt and pepper. Stir in mussels, 1 cup blanched corn, zucchini, carrot and bell pepper. Garnish with cilantro leaves. Serve immediately.

New England Seafood Chowder

Tomatoes add a nice touch of color and flavor to this soup.

6 servings

6 ounces bacon (about 8 slices), cut into 1-inch squares
4 medium-large onions, coarsely chopped
3 medium celery stalks, sliced
3 pounds boiling potatoes, peeled and cut into ½-inch cubes
3 cups Fish Stock* or two 8-ounce bottles clam juice mixed with 1 cup water
Additional Fish Stock or water
2 thyme sprigs or ¼ teaspoon dried, crumbled
3 parsley sprigs

2 cups (or more) milk
½ cup whipping cream
Hot pepper sauce (optional)
Salt and freshly ground pepper
2 pounds scrod, cod or haddock fillets, cut into 1½-inch cubes
1¼ cups drained canned tomatoes, cut into ¾-inch pieces
8 ounces whole bay scallops or sea scallops, cut into 3 pieces each
Unsalted butter
Paprika

Cook bacon in heavy Dutch oven over medium heat until golden brown, stirring frequently, 8 to 10 minutes. Transfer to paper towel using slotted spoon. Pour off all but 3 tablespoons bacon fat. Add onions and celery to Dutch oven. Cover and cook over medium-low heat, stirring occasionally, until slightly softened, about 10 minutes. Add potatoes, 3 cups fish stock and additional fish stock or water if necessary to almost cover vegetables. Bring to boil. Tie thyme and parsley in piece of cheesecloth. Add to soup. Reduce heat, cover and simmer until potatoes are just tender, 15 to 20 minutes.

Transfer half of vegetables to processor or food mill using slotted spoon. Puree until smooth. Return puree to soup. Add 2 cups milk, cream, pepper sauce to taste, salt and generous amount of pepper. Bring soup to boil, stirring until smooth. Thin with more milk if desired. Add fish. Cover and simmer until fish is almost opaque, 2 to 3 minutes. Discard cheesecloth bag. Add tomatoes, scallops and bacon to soup; stir gently to avoid breaking fish. Adjust seasoning. Cover and simmer until fish and scallops are just opaque, about 1 minute. Ladle soup into bowls. Top each with thin pat of butter. Sprinkle with paprika and serve.

*Fish Stock

Makes 6 cups

1 tablespoon butter	1½ cups dry white wine
1 medium onion, sliced	¼ lemon
1 medium leek, halved lengthwise and sliced	2 thyme sprigs or ½ teaspoon dried, crumbled
1 medium celery stalk, sliced	1 bay leaf
3 pounds bones and heads from nonoily fish, such as flounder, cod and halibut (gills removed), rinsed and coarsely chopped	½ teaspoon salt

Melt butter in heavy large nonaluminum pot over low heat. Add onion, leek and celery. Cover and cook until beginning to soften, stirring occasionally, about 8 minutes. Add fish bones. Cover and cook 5 minutes, stirring occasionally. Add wine, lemon, thyme, bay leaf, salt and enough water to cover. Bring to boil, skimming surface occasionally. Reduce heat and simmer 25 minutes. Strain. Return stock to clean pot. Boil until reduced to 6 cups. Degrease. (*Can be prepared 2 days ahead and refrigerated or frozen 3 months.*)

Crab and Vegetable Soup

Vary the ingredients according to what you have on hand.

Makes about 5 quarts

1 pound flanken, top rib or beef ribs	1 3-ounce can corn, drained
8 ounces soup bones	2½ ounces frozen peas
10 to 11 cups water	3 tomatoes, chopped, or one 14-ounce can tomatoes, undrained
1 large onion, chopped	
2 celery stalks, diced	3 beef bouillon cubes
3 carrots, diced	1 teaspoon Old Bay seafood seasoning
½ cup baby lima beans, rinsed	
¼ cup split peas	1 teaspoon salt
¼ cup barley	½ teaspoon freshly ground pepper
1½ large potatoes, peeled and diced	6 ounces fresh or frozen crabmeat
1½ zucchini, diced	
¾ cup green beans, broken into thirds	

Rinse beef ribs and transfer to heavy large stockpot. Add bones and 6 cups water. Bring to boil over high heat, skimming foam from surface as necessary. Reduce heat to medium-high. Add onion and celery and cook 15 minutes, skimming foam from surface again if necessary. Add carrot, lima beans, split peas and barley and continue cooking on medium-high heat 20 minutes. Skim again if necessary. Add potato, zucchini, green beans, corn and peas. Stir in remaining 4 to 5 cups water, depending on desired thickness. Continue cooking on medium-high heat 30 minutes. Add tomatoes and juice, bouillon cubes, seafood seasoning, salt and pepper. Reduce heat to low and cook, stirring occasionally, until vegetables are tender, about 30 minutes.

Discard soup bones. Remove beef ribs and let cool. Cut meat from ribs and return to soup. Add crabmeat and heat just until cooked through (or warmed through if frozen), about 2 to 3 minutes. Taste and adjust seasoning and serve.

Ajiaco Bogotano (Colombian Chicken and Potato Soup)

This soup makes wonderful party food because guests get involved in passing the condiments and creating new combinations of flavors.

12 servings

12 cups water
5 pounds baking potatoes, peeled and coarsely chopped
5 pounds boiling potatoes, peeled and coarsely chopped
1 3- to 4-pound frying chicken
1 large onion, sliced

Salt and freshly ground pepper
2 17-ounce cans sweet corn, drained
2 cups sour cream
6 medium avocados, sliced
2 3¼-ounce jars capers, drained

Combine water, potatoes, chicken and onion in stockpot. Bring to boil over medium-high heat. Cover and simmer until potatoes are soft and chicken is tender when pierced with tip of knife, about 40 minutes.

Reduce heat to low. Remove chicken and let cool slightly. Separate meat from bones and chop into bite-size pieces; discard skin and bones. Transfer chicken to small dish. Degrease soup if necessary. Season with salt and pepper. Ladle into bowls and serve. Pass chopped chicken, corn, sour cream, avocados and capers as condiments.

Hearty Turkey and Vegetable Soup

Save the carcass, pan juices and any leftover gravy from your next turkey for the broth for this soup.

6 to 8 servings

Turkey Broth
2 tablespoons (¼ stick) butter
1 cooked turkey carcass,* chopped
1 large onion with skin, coarsely chopped
1 large carrot, coarsely chopped
1 celery stalk, coarsely chopped
2 medium garlic cloves, crushed
4 juniper berries, crushed
  Pinch of fresh or dried thyme, crumbled
6 cups chicken stock, degreased
1 medium tomato or 2 canned tomatoes, drained, coarsely chopped
  Turkey gravy (if available)
  Pan juices (if available)

Soup
2 medium boiling potatoes, peeled and sliced
1 large celery root, peeled, quartered and sliced
2 medium carrots, peeled and sliced diagonally
1 to 2 cups diced cooked turkey meat* (if available)
1 celery stalk, sliced diagonally
1 cup thickly sliced mushrooms
3 tablespoons minced fresh parsley
  Salt and freshly ground pepper

For broth: Melt butter in heavy Dutch oven over medium-high heat. Add turkey carcass and brown lightly, stirring occasionally, about 8 minutes. Add onion, carrot, celery, garlic, juniper berries and thyme. Cook until vegetables soften, stirring frequently, about 10 minutes. Add chicken stock, tomato, gravy and pan juices. Bring to boil, skimming surface. Reduce heat, cover partially and simmer 2 hours. Strain broth. Return to clean pan.

For soup: Add potatoes and celery root to broth. Boil gently until tender, about 20 minutes. Transfer vegetables to processor using slotted spoon. Puree until smooth. Add carrots to broth. Cover partially and simmer 5 minutes. Whisk in potato-celery root puree. Add turkey meat, celery and mushrooms. Cover partially and simmer 10 minutes. (*Can be prepared 1 day ahead and refrigerated. Bring to simmer before continuing.*) Mix in 2 tablespoons parsley. Season with salt and pepper. Ladle soup into heated bowls. Sprinkle with remaining 1 tablespoon minced parsley and serve.

*If unavailable, turkey breast and 2 drumsticks can be substituted. After simmering in broth, reserve meat for soup.

Potée d'Ardennes

A fresh interpretation of the rustic soup-stew from southeastern Belgium. Best if made one to two days ahead and allowed to mellow in the refrigerator. Serve in heated soup bowls with lots of coarse country bread, butter and beer.

8 to 10 servings

4 ounces lean bacon (preferably deep-smoked country bacon), chopped
2 tablespoons (¼ stick) butter
5 to 6 medium onions, chopped (about 6 cups)
3 cups coarsely chopped peeled celery root* (about 1⅓ pounds)
4 medium carrots, coarsely chopped (about 1 generous cup)
6 cups (about) chopped green cabbage (about 1½ pounds)
2 to 3 pounds smoked ham hocks or 1 meaty ham bone, cut into several pieces

¼ cup chopped fresh parsley
3 large white rose potatoes, peeled and coarsely chopped (about 1¼ pounds)
6 to 8 cups chicken, veal or beef stock, preferably homemade

8 to 12 ounces knackwurst (preferably lightly smoked), cut into bite-size pieces
8 to 12 ounces green beans, cut into 1-inch pieces
Salt and freshly ground pepper

Combine bacon and butter in heavy nonaluminum 10- to 12-quart stockpot over medium-low heat and cook until bacon is translucent. Spoon off all but about 4 tablespoons of fat. Add onion and cook until soft and translucent, about 10 minutes, stirring occasionally. Stir in celery root and carrot and cook 15 minutes, stirring occasionally. Add cabbage, ham hocks and parsley and cook 15 minutes. Add potatoes with enough stock to cover all ingredients. Increase heat and bring to boil. Reduce heat until mixture barely simmers. Cover stockpot partially and simmer soup gently for 2 hours.

Remove ham hocks with slotted spoon. Set aside until cool enough to handle. Remove meat; shred into small pieces. Add meat to soup. Press marrow from bones into soup. Add knackwurst and green beans. Simmer gently until mixture is consistency of thick soup, 45 minutes to 1 hour. Season with salt and pepper. Ladle into heated bowls. Serve immediately. (*Soup can be prepared 1 to 2 days ahead and refrigerated. Degrease surface of soup before reheating.*)

*If celery root is unavailable, substitute 2 celery stalks, chopped, mixed with enough chopped turnip to equal 3 cups total.

Mongolian Hot Pot, Shanghai Style

Enjoy this spectacular one-dish meal by removing tidbits from the pot with chopsticks and dipping them into the sauce. After you finish the main ingredients, ladle the broth into individual bowls for a flavorful ending. An electric skillet can replace the hot pot.

6 main-course servings or 8 servings as part of multi-course Chinese meal

Chicken Broth
1½ pounds chicken pieces
10 cups water
2 tablespoons salt

Meatballs
2 pounds freshly ground pork
1 tablespoon cornstarch
1 tablespoon minced fresh ginger
1½ teaspoons salt
⅛ teaspoon freshly ground white pepper
⅛ teaspoon Chinese cooking wine or dry white wine
Several drops of oriental sesame oil

Rolled Omelets
6 eggs
1 teaspoon salt
1 tablespoon vegetable oil

Cornstarch

3 ounces bean thread noodles
8 medium Chinese dried black mushrooms
8 large unshelled prawns

1½ pounds Chinese cabbage (*siu choy*), halved lengthwise, cored and cut into 1½-inch squares
1 8- to 10-ounce package Japanese fish balls (do not use frozen)
12 ounces ½-inch-thick ham steaks, cut into wedges
1 5- to 8-ounce package Japanese fried fish cakes (do not use frozen), cut into ⅛-inch slices
5 green onions, cut into 2-inch lengths and ends fringed to resemble flowers

Salt (optional)
Sesame-Soy Dipping Sauce*

For broth: Place chicken in large saucepan. Add 10 cups water. Bring to boil, skimming foam from surface. Reduce heat, cover and simmer 3 hours. Discard chicken. Season broth with salt. (*Broth can be prepared 1 day ahead. Cover tightly and refrigerate.*)

For meatballs: Mix pork, cornstarch, ginger, salt, pepper, wine and sesame oil vigorously with wooden spoon 3 minutes. Scoop up 30 portions of meat mixture using large end of melon baller. Roll into 1½-inch balls. Arrange in single layer on heatproof plate. Set remainder aside.

For omelets: Beat eggs with salt to blend. Heat vegetable oil in wok or heavy 10- to 12-inch skillet over medium-high heat. Pour in half of eggs, tilting wok to spread mixture 5 inches up sides. Cook until eggs are set, about 2 minutes. Turn with spatula and cook 1 minute. Remove. Repeat with remaining eggs. Cool omelets completely.

Dust browned side of omelets with cornstarch. Divide remaining pork mixture among omelets, smoothing gently with knife, leaving ½-inch border. Roll up tightly jelly roll style. Place on heatproof plate.

Bring water to rapid boil in steamer over high heat. Set plate with meatballs on steamer rack. Cover and steam until cooked through, about 10 minutes. Remove meatballs and set plate with omelets on steamer rack. Cover and steam until cooked through, about 15 minutes. Cool meatballs and omelets to room temperature. Cover omelets and refrigerate at least 30 minutes. (*Omelets and meatballs can be prepared up to 1 day ahead. Cover and refrigerate. Bring to room temperature before using.*)

Soak bean thread noodles in bowl of lukewarm water to cover at least 1 hour. Soak black mushrooms in bowl of lukewarm water to cover until soft, about 30 minutes. Meanwhile, devein prawns by cutting down backs through shell and flesh. Wash prawns and pat dry. Drain noodles. Drain mushrooms; discard stems. Rinse and squeeze out excess moisture.

To assemble: Heat charcoal in barbecue to white coals. Spread out cabbage in hot pot pan. Top with noodles. Mound fish balls in one section of pan. Place meatballs on opposite side. Cut omelet rolls into ¾-inch slices. Arrange omelet rolls, ham, mushrooms and fish cakes in pan in groups, separating each with green onion flower. Place prawns on top. Heat chicken broth to simmering.

Gently pour broth into pot to ½ inch from top, adding boiling water if necessary. Add salt if desired. Cover pot. Place on baking sheet set atop wooden board in center of table. Add hot coals to brazier using tongs. Bring broth to boil. Serve with dipping sauce.

To prepare in electric skillet: Arrange half of all ingredients in skillet. Cover and bring to boil. Reduce heat to simmer and serve. Add remaining ingredients as needed.

*Sesame-Soy Dipping Sauce

Makes about ¾ cup

½ cup dark soy sauce
4½ tablespoons light soy sauce
¾ teaspoon oriental sesame oil

¾ teaspoon Chinese chili sauce (optional)

Mix all ingredients in small bowl.

Portuguese Green Soup

A hearty, potato-based soup from the Minho province north of Porto. Serve with corn bread for a delicious main course. Kale, spinach, turnip or mustard greens can be substituted for collards.

6 to 8 servings

4 tablespoons olive oil
1 medium onion, minced
6 large boiling potatoes, peeled and thinly sliced
2 quarts cold water

6 ounces linguiça or other dry garlic sausage (such as chorizo or pepperoni), thinly sliced

2½ teaspoons salt
¼ teaspoon freshly ground pepper
1 pound collards, coarse stems and veins removed, leaves rolled up and cut into thin strips

Heat 3 tablespoons oil in heavy large saucepan over medium heat. Add onion and stir until just beginning to color, about 3 minutes. Add potatoes and stir until just beginning to color, about 3 minutes. Pour in water. Cover tightly and boil gently until potatoes are very tender, 20 to 25 minutes.

Cook sausage in heavy medium skillet over low heat until most of fat has been rendered, 10 to 12 minutes. Remove and drain on paper towels.

Remove potatoes from heat. Mash in saucepan using straight up and down motion to prevent stickiness. Add sausage, salt and pepper. Cover and simmer over medium heat 5 minutes to blend flavors. Add collards, cover and simmer until crisp-tender, about 5 minutes. Stir in remaining 1 tablespoon oil. Adjust seasoning. Ladle soup into bowls and serve.

Sausage Garbure

This lusty mélange of dried beans, vegetables and meat was born in Béarn, in France's southwest corner, and spread from there to the Basque country and Gascony. In each area, subtle differences have developed. For example, Basque cooks are likely to include a chunk of salt pork, while in Béarn preserved goose is the meat of choice. But ham, bacon and sausage are the meats most often found in homemade garbure.

The rituals surrounding this dish also seem to change from region to region, but in most areas the meat is taken from the soup, sliced and served separately. The broth and vegetables are then ladled onto a crisp croûte and, traditionally, a little red wine is poured into the soup just before it is eaten.

2 servings

3 cups water
¼ cup dried Great Northern or navy beans

1 1-pound smoked ham hock
1 small turnip (4 to 5 ounces), peeled and diced
1 medium carrot, sliced
1 medium celery stalk, sliced
½ small onion, sliced
2 garlic cloves, minced
1 parsley sprig
½ bay leaf
   Pinch *each* of dried marjoram, dried thyme and dried red pepper flakes
8 ounces cabbage, shredded

½ cup (3 ounces) peeled, diced boiling potato

4 ounces kielbasa, chorizo or cotechino sausage
4 ounces fresh fava beans (about 4), shelled, or 1 ounce shelled fava or lima beans
2 ounces fresh peas, shelled (2 to 3 tablespoons)
   Salt and freshly ground pepper

Croûtes
2 ¾- to 1-inch-thick slices French bread
1 tablespoon olive oil

2 tablespoons minced fresh parsley

Combine water and dried beans in large saucepan and bring to boil over high heat. Let boil 2 minutes. Remove from heat, cover and let stand 1 hour (or soak beans overnight without boiling).

Add ham hock, turnip, carrot, celery, onion, garlic, herbs and pepper flakes to beans and bring to boil. Reduce heat, cover partially and simmer 45 minutes. Add cabbage and potato and continue cooking until vegetables are tender, about 45 minutes. (*Can be prepared ahead to this point, cooled and refrigerated.*)

Prick sausage in several places with fork. Add to soup with fava beans and peas and cook 30 minutes, adding more water if soup is too thick. Season to taste with salt and pepper.

Meanwhile, prepare croûtes: Preheat oven to 325°F. Arrange bread slices in single layer on baking sheet. Bake 15 minutes. Brush both sides with olive oil; turn slices over. Bake 15 more minutes.

To serve, remove ham hock and sausage. Discard bone and tendon from hock; cut meat into bite-size pieces. Cut sausage into long diagonal slices. Return meats to soup or serve separately on heated platter. Place 1 croûte in bottom of each heated bowl. Ladle soup over top. Sprinkle with parsley and serve.

2 🍎 *Savory Pies*

======================

Ever since Americans discovered quiche, main-dish pies have been enjoying a seemingly boundless surge in popularity. It is no wonder that the classic quiche Lorraine has so many rivals these days, for a savory pie or tart is an easy and attractive one-dish meal.

This chapter offers an array of many crusts and even more fillings, divided into groups emphasizing vegetables and cheese, fish, poultry and meat. Perfect as a meatless lunch or supper entrée is Carrot Pie (page 16), Fresh Vegetable Pie (page 17), or hearty English-style Cheese and Onion Pie (page 21). Among the fish- and meat-filled selections, the choices range from suave, puff-pastry-wrapped Tourte de la Vallée de Munster (page 31) to a fast-to-fix Salmon-Zucchini Quiche (page 22).

Since main-dish pastries crop up in many of the world's cuisines, you will find a generous sampling of international favorites here. Savory Pie of Five Cheeses (page 21) and olive-studded Spinach and Raisin Pie (page 19) are strictly Italian. Where winters are long and cold, however, cooks seem to be even more partial to savory pastries. Scandinavia offers Helsinki Vegetable Pie (page 17), Karelian Rice and Rye Pasties (page 20), Quail Pies (page 24), and Ham Piirakka (page 32); Russians dote on Lamb and Onion Pirog (page 28); and pork *Tourtière* (page 30) is one of French Canada's most beloved and characteristic dishes.

So look to this chapter for ideas, whether you need a picnic take-along or buffet showpiece. One savory pie or another will be exactly right.

🍎 Vegetable and Cheese Pies

Carrot Pie

8 to 10 servings

Whole Wheat Pastry
1½ cups all purpose flour
½ cup whole wheat flour
1 teaspoon salt
½ cup (1 stick) chilled unsalted butter, cut into small pieces
2 tablespoons chilled lard or solid vegetable shortening
2 to 4 tablespoons ice water
1 egg
1 tablespoon distilled white or cider vinegar

Carrot Filling
7 tablespoons unsalted butter
1 large onion, thinly sliced

2 pounds carrots, peeled and shredded
¼ cup water
2 eggs
2 egg yolks
1 teaspoon salt
½ teaspoon ground allspice
½ teaspoon freshly ground white pepper

1 cup freshly cooked brown rice
1 cup shredded Emmenthal cheese
1 egg beaten with 2 tablespoons milk (glaze)

For pastry: Combine flours and salt in large bowl. Cut in butter and lard until mixture resembles coarse meal. Beat 2 tablespoons ice water, egg and vinegar to blend. Mix into flour just until dough comes together in ball. If dough seems dry, add up to 2 tablespoons more water a few drops at a time. Wrap dough in plastic and chill 1 hour.

For filling: Melt 4 tablespoons butter in heavy small skillet over low heat. Add onion, cover and cook until soft, stirring occasionally, about 10 minutes. Remove from skillet. Melt remaining 3 tablespoons butter in same skillet over low heat. Add carrots, increase heat to high and stir 2 minutes. Reduce heat to low. Add water, cover and cook until carrots are tender and liquid is absorbed, about 20 minutes (if carrots are tender and liquid remains, drain carrots). Puree onion and carrots in processor with eggs, yolks, salt, allspice and pepper until smooth. Turn into bowl. Refrigerate 1 hour.

To assemble: Preheat oven to 325°F. Grease 5½ × 9½-inch or 4½ × 11-inch loaf pan. Roll dough out on lightly floured surface to thickness of ¼ inch. Cut out 12 × 16-inch rectangle. Drape dough loosely in pan. Press dough into corners with fingers. Trim dough flush with top. Roll scraps out to thickness of ¼ inch. Cut out rectangle large enough to form cover for pie.

Stir rice and cheese into carrot mixture. Spoon into prepared pan. Brush edge of crust with glaze. Cover with remaining rectangle of dough, pressing to seal. Roll remaining scraps out. Cut out decorations and affix with glaze. Brush entire pie with glaze. If any scraps remain, cut out strips to fit around top edge of pie. Snip or poke 8 air holes on top of pie. Bake until pastry is lightly browned and instant-reading thermometer registers 160°F in center of pie and 165°F around edges, about 1½ hours. Cool in pan on rack. Carefully remove loaf from pan. Serve at room temperature.

Fresh Vegetable Pie

6 to 8 servings

2 tablespoons vegetable oil
2 garlic cloves, chopped
3 medium tomatoes, cored and chopped
2 small onions, chopped
1 small eggplant, peeled, quartered and sliced
1 small green bell pepper, seeded and sliced

1 cup fresh or frozen corn kernels
Salt and freshly ground pepper
3 medium zucchini, sliced
6 tablespoons freshly grated Parmesan cheese
1 unbaked 9-inch pie crust
2 tablespoons (1/4 stick) butter, cut into pieces

Preheat oven to 350°F. Heat oil and garlic in large skillet over medium-high heat. Add tomatoes, onion, eggplant, green pepper, corn, salt and pepper and sauté until vegetables are crisp-tender, about 7 minutes. Stir in zucchini and continue cooking until zucchini is crisp-tender. Sprinkle 2 tablespoons cheese over bottom of pie crust. Add half of vegetables using slotted spoon. Sprinkle with 2 tablespoons cheese and dot with 1 tablespoon butter. Add remaining vegetables, sprinkle with remaining cheese and dot with butter. Bake until crust is golden brown, about 40 minutes. Serve hot.

Helsinki Vegetable Pie

6 to 8 servings

Sour Cream Pastry
1 1/2 cups all purpose flour
2 teaspoons baking powder
1 teaspoon salt
1/2 cup (1 stick) chilled unsalted butter, cut into small pieces
1 cup sour cream

Mixed Vegetable Filling
7 tablespoons butter
2 cups shredded carrot
1 cup shredded parsnip
1/2 cup sliced green onion
2 garlic cloves, minced
6 cups finely shredded green cabbage

2 cups shredded Emmenthal or Gruyère cheese
1 1/2 cups freshly cooked brown rice
1/4 cup minced fresh parsley
1/4 cup whipping cream
1 teaspoon salt
1 teaspoon dried oregano, crumbled
Pinch of freshly grated nutmeg
Pinch of ground allspice

1 egg, beaten with 2 tablespoons milk (glaze)

For pastry: Combine flour, baking powder and salt in large bowl. Cut in butter until mixture resembles coarse meal. Stir in sour cream until stiff dough forms. Gather into ball. Wrap in plastic and refrigerate 30 minutes.

For filling: Melt 3 tablespoons butter in heavy large saucepan over medium heat. Add carrot, parsnip, green onion and garlic and stir 5 minutes. Add cabbage and stir until wilted, about 5 minutes. Transfer to large bowl. Cool to room temperature, about 10 minutes. Blend in cheese, rice, parsley, cream, salt, oregano, nutmeg and allspice.

To assemble: Preheat oven to 400°F. Grease 10-inch metal pie pan. Roll out 3/4 of dough on lightly floured surface into 12-inch circle. Fit into prepared pan. Trim and form edges. Spoon in filling, spreading evenly. Dot with remaining butter. Roll out remaining 1/4 of dough into 11-inch circle. Cut into 1/2-inch strips using fluted pastry cutter. Brush edge of pie shell with egg glaze. Arrange half of strips diagonally across top of pie, spacing about ¾ inch apart. Arrange remaining strips diagonally in opposite direction, spacing about ¾ inch apart. Trim strips, pressing ends into edge. Press any extra strips around edge of pie to form border. Brush strips with egg glaze. Bake pie until pastry browns, about 45 minutes. Serve immediately.

Winter Vegetable Tourte

Delicious hot or just warm and an ideal centerpiece dish for a special buffet. A first course might be a light consommé, with fresh fruit or a sorbet for dessert. Pour a crisp Johannisberg Riesling.

8 to 10 servings

Pastry
2½ cups unbleached all purpose flour
½ cup cake flour
¼ teaspoon salt
12 tablespoons (1½ sticks) chilled unsalted butter, cut into small pieces
2 eggs, beaten to blend

Filling
2½ pounds fresh spinach, stemmed, or two 10-ounce packages frozen, thawed, squeezed dry and chopped

2 tablespoons (¼ stick) butter
4 ounces smoked ham (fat trimmed and reserved), thinly sliced and cut into 2-inch squares
6 large shallots, minced (about 1 cup)

12 ounces Swiss chard (hard cores removed), minced and cooked until barely tender
⅓ cup raisins
¼ cup dry vermouth

12 ounces cream cheese, room temperature
2 egg yolks
1 egg
½ cup coarsely chopped walnuts
Pinch of freshly grated nutmeg
Pinch of dried rosemary, crumbled
Salt and freshly ground pepper
6 ounces Gruyère cheese, thinly sliced
1 egg beaten with 1 teaspoon water (glaze)

For pastry: Combine flours and salt in processor and mix several seconds. Add butter and mix using on/off turns until mixture resembles coarse meal. Add beaten eggs and mix using on/off turns until mixture just clings together; do not form ball. Gather dough into ball. Wrap tightly in plastic and flatten into disc. Refrigerate overnight or freeze up to 1 month. (Bring almost to room temperature before rolling.)

For filling: Rinse fresh spinach well. Shake off excess water. Transfer spinach to large saucepan. Cover and cook over medium-high heat, turning spinach occasionally just until wilted, 2 to 3 minutes. Drain spinach in colander, pressing out as much liquid as possible. Squeeze dry; chop and set aside.

Melt butter in heavy large nonaluminum skillet over medium heat. Add reserved ham fat and cook until melted. Add ham and cook 30 seconds. Remove ham with slotted spoon and set aside. Stir in shallot and cook until soft. Increase heat, add Swiss chard, raisins and spinach and cook until most of moisture has evaporated. Stir in vermouth and cook until evaporated. Set aside to cool.

Combine cream cheese, egg yolks and egg in large bowl and mix until smooth. Add walnuts, nutmeg, rosemary and vegetable mixture. Season with salt and pepper and mix well. Taste and adjust seasoning. (*Filling can be prepared 1 day ahead and refrigerated.*)

To assemble: Grease 12-inch pizza pan. Divide dough in half. Roll 1 piece out between 2 sheets of waxed paper into circle about ⅛ inch thick. Trim to 14-inch circle; reserve scraps. Transfer circle to prepared pizza pan. Spread half of filling over pastry, leaving 1½-inch border all around. Top with overlapping slices of cheese. Sprinkle with ham. Spread remaining filling over top. Brush border with egg mixture.

Roll remaining piece of dough out between 2 sheets of waxed paper into circle about ⅛ inch thick. Trim to slightly larger than 14-inch circle; reserve scraps. Arrange pastry over filling. Press edges together and roll upward toward center to seal. Crimp edges decoratively. Brush top with egg mixture. Reroll reserved scraps about ⅛ inch thick. Cut pastry into spinach-leaf patterns of varying sizes. Using tip of sharp knife, etch leaf vein pattern into pastry leaves. Cut 1½-inch-diameter hole in center of tourte. Arrange pastry leaves decoratively around hole and over top. Brush leaves with egg glaze.

Preheat oven to 450°F. Bake tourte 20 minutes. Reduce oven temperature to 375°F and continue baking until knife inserted in center comes out clean, about 1 hour. Serve hot or warm.

Vegetable tourte can be prepared ahead and reheated in 325°F oven.

Italian Spinach and Raisin Pie (Pitta di Spinaci)

A superb main course.

6 to 8 servings

Spinach Filling
2½ pounds spinach, stemmed

¼ cup olive oil
¼ cup minced onion
3 garlic cloves, minced
6 ounces black olives (preferably Kalamata), pitted and cut into ⅓-inch pieces
½ cup raisins
¼ to ½ teaspoon dried red pepper flakes
Freshly ground pepper

Yeast Crust
2 envelopes dry yeast
1½ cups warm water (105°F to 115°F)
4½ cups unbleached all purpose flour

3 tablespoons olive oil
1 tablespoon salt

12 ounces mozzarella cheese (preferably fresh), shredded
6 tablespoons olive oil

For filling: Rinse spinach; shake off excess water. Transfer to Dutch oven. Cover and cook over low heat, stirring frequently, until just wilted, about 3 minutes. Rinse with cold water and squeeze dry. Chop coarsely.

Heat oil in heavy large skillet over low heat. Add onion and garlic and cook until soft, about 10 minutes. Mix in olives and raisins and cook 2 minutes, stirring frequently. Add spinach, red pepper flakes and pepper. Stir 5 minutes. (*Filling can be prepared 1 day ahead. Cover and refrigerate. Bring to room temperature before continuing with recipe.*)

For crust: Sprinkle yeast over ½ cup warm water in small bowl; stir to dissolve. Arrange 1½ cups flour in mound on work surface and make well in center. Add yeast to well. Using fork, gradually draw flour from inner edge of well into center until all flour is incorporated. Knead sponge until smooth and elastic, 8 to 10 minutes. (Can also be prepared in processor. Knead 1 minute.) Lightly flour large bowl and add sponge. Cover with towel. Let sponge rise in warm draft-free area until doubled, about 2 hours.

Arrange remaining 3 cups flour in mound on work surface and make well in center. Add raised sponge to well and pull to form well in sponge. Add remaining 1 cup water, 3 tablespoons oil and salt to well in sponge. Knead mixtures together until smooth and elastic dough forms, 8 to 10 minutes. (Can also be prepared in processor. Knead 1 minute.) Return to floured bowl. Cover with towel. Let dough rise in draft-free area until doubled in volume, about 1½ hours.

Mix cheese with 1 tablespoon oil. Add salt and pepper to taste.

Preheat oven to 400°F. Spread 3 tablespoons oil in bottom of 9 × 13-inch metal baking pan. Punch dough down. Cut into 2 pieces, one 1½ times larger than the other. Roll large piece out on lightly floured surface into 11 × 15-inch rectangle. Fit dough into prepared pan, covering bottom and sides. Brush with remaining 2 tablespoons oil.

Spread filling in pan and sprinkle with cheese. Roll remaining dough out on lightly floured surface into 9 × 13-inch rectangle. Brush edges with water and place atop filling. Pinch top and bottom crusts together. Brush top of pie with water. Cut three 3-inch slits in top. Bake until well browned, about 35 minutes. Cool slightly. Serve pie warm or at room temperature.

Karelian Rice and Rye Pasties

Makes 32

Creamy Rice Filling
1 cup water
1 cup medium-grain rice
4 cups (1 quart) milk
2 tablespoons (¼ stick) butter
2 teaspoons salt

Rye Pastry
1 cup hot water
¼ cup (½ stick) butter, melted
1 teaspoon salt

1½ cups all purpose flour
1½ cups medium rye flour

½ cup (1 stick) butter, melted, blended with ½ cup hot milk (glaze)
Egg Butter*

For filling: Bring water and rice to boil in heavy medium saucepan. Stir once and cover. Reduce heat to low and cook until all liquid is absorbed, about 10 minutes. Stir in 2 cups milk and cook uncovered until all milk is absorbed, stirring frequently. Stir in 1 cup milk. Cook until all liquid is absorbed, stirring frequently. Repeat with remaining cup of milk. Blend in 2 tablespoons butter and 2 teaspoons salt; cool to room temperature.

For pastry: Combine water, ¼ cup butter and 1 teaspoon salt in large bowl. Add all purpose flour and stir until smooth. Add 1 cup rye flour and stir until stiff. Let stand 15 minutes.

To assemble: Preheat oven to 450°F. Line baking sheets with parchment paper. Stir ¼ cup of remaining rye flour into dough. Turn dough out onto work surface and knead until smooth. Divide dough into fourths; cut each fourth into 8 pieces. Shape each piece into ball. Sprinkle remaining ¼ cup rye flour onto surface. Roll each ball into 4- to 5-inch circle. Set circles on prepared sheets. Spoon generous tablespoon of filling in center of each circle, spreading to within ½ inch of edges. Fold opposite sides of dough over filling to meet in center. Crimp short ends to make oval shape with filling exposed in center. Brush each oval generously with glaze. Bake until golden, 15 to 18 minutes. Brush again with glaze. Serve pasties with egg butter.

*Egg Butter

This accompaniment to the Karelian Rice and Rye Pasties is also excellent when simply spread on toast.

Makes 2 cups

1 cup (2 sticks) butter, room temperature
¼ teaspoon salt

¼ teaspoon ground ginger
4 hard-cooked eggs, chopped

Beat butter until light. Add salt and ginger. Blend in hard-cooked eggs. Pack into small bowl and refrigerate. Serve butter at room temperature.

Cheese and Onion Pie

6 to 8 servings

Short Crust Pastry
2 cups all purpose flour
½ cup solid vegetable shortening
3 tablespoons (or more) ice water
1 teaspoon salt

Filling
4 tablespoons (½ stick) butter
2 medium onions, thinly sliced
Salt and freshly ground pepper

2 medium baking potatoes, peeled and thinly sliced

12 ounces sharp cheddar cheese, grated
1 egg beaten with 2 tablespoons milk (glaze)

For pastry: Beat ¼ cup flour, ½ cup shortening, 3 tablespoons ice water and salt in large bowl with large whisk or wooden spoon. Using fingertips, blend in remaining 1¾ cups flour until mixture resembles coarse meal. If too dry, add up to 1 tablespoon more ice water a few drops at a time. Gather dough into ball. Cover with damp towel. Refrigerate at least 1 hour.

For filling: Melt 2 tablespoons butter in heavy large skillet over medium heat. Add onions and stir until soft but not brown, about 8 minutes. Season with salt and pepper. Cool to room temperature.

Halve potato slices. Melt remaining 2 tablespoons butter in another heavy large skillet over medium heat. Add potatoes and cook until crisp-tender, turning occasionally, 10 to 15 minutes. Season with salt and pepper to taste. Let cool to room temperature.

Preheat oven to 350°F. Grease 10-inch deep-dish pie plate. Divide dough in half. Return half to refrigerator. Roll remainder out on lightly floured surface into circle ⅛ inch thick. Fit into prepared pie plate; trim edges. Add half of cheese, leaving ½-inch border. Top with half of onions, then half of potatoes. Repeat layering with remaining ingredients. Roll remaining half of dough out into circle ⅛ inch thick. Brush rim of shell with some of egg glaze. Cover pie with dough circle; trim and flute edges. Brush generously with egg glaze. Bake until pastry is golden brown, about 30 minutes. Serve pie hot or at room temperature.

Savory Pie of Five Cheeses

4 to 6 servings

Dough
1½ cups all purpose flour
1 teaspoon salt
1½ teaspoons dry yeast dissolved in
    1 tablespoon warm water (110°F)
1 tablespoon olive oil
⅓ to ½ cup water

Topping
3 red bell peppers
Olive oil

4 ounces pancetta, cut into slivers
1 tablespoon olive oil
1 red onion, thinly sliced
2 garlic cloves, sliced
Salt and freshly ground pepper
Freshly grated nutmeg

8 ounces ricotta cheese
½ cup grated mozzarella cheese
½ cup freshly grated Parmesan cheese
¼ cup grated provolone cheese
¼ cup grated pecorino cheese
2 tablespoons whipping cream
2 tablespoons sour cream
2 eggs
¼ cup minced Italian parsley

For dough: Mix flour and salt on work surface. Make well in center. Add dissolved yeast and oil. Stir in ⅓ cup water with fork. With fingertips, gradually blend in flour from border of well (if all flour is not incorporated, make well in remaining flour and work in a little more water). Knead dough until no longer sticky, 10 minutes. Transfer to greased bowl, turning to coat entire surface. Cover and let stand in warm draft-free area until doubled in volume, about 1½ to 2 hours.

Punch dough down. Let rise a second time until doubled in volume.

For topping: Rub peppers with thin coating of olive oil. Char over gas flame or under broiler, turning until skins blister and blacken. Steam in plastic bag 10 minutes. Peel off skins; cut into quarters and remove seeds.

Cook pancetta in heavy medium skillet over medium heat until golden, about 5 minutes. Remove with slotted spoon and drain on paper towels. Discard all but 1 tablespoon fat. Add 1 tablespoon olive oil to skillet and reheat over medium heat. Stir in onion and garlic and sauté until just brown. Add salt, pepper and nutmeg. Cool.

Mix cheeses, creams, eggs, parsley and pancetta into cooled onion mixture. Season with salt, pepper and nutmeg.

Punch dough down. Fit into 10-inch pie dish. Pour in filling. Decorate top of pie with red pepper quarters.

Position rack in lowest part of oven and preheat to 375°F. Bake pie until filling is set and browned, about 20 minutes (if filling is not set, transfer to center rack and bake 10 more minutes). Cool 10 minutes before serving.

❦ Fish, Poultry and Meat Pies

Salmon-Zucchini Quiche

4 to 6 servings

1 unbaked 9-inch deep-dish pie crust
1 egg white, lightly beaten
1 tablespoon butter
1½ cups thinly sliced zucchini
½ cup chopped onion
1 7¾-ounce can salmon (liquid reserved, skin and bones discarded), flaked

⅔ cup grated Swiss cheese
3 eggs
1½ cups half and half
½ teaspoon salt
1 teaspoon minced fresh dill or ¼ teaspoon dried dillweed
Freshly ground pepper

Preheat oven to 375°F. Brush pie crust with egg white. Melt butter in medium skillet over medium-high heat. Add zucchini and onion and sauté until crisp-tender, about 2 minutes. Let cool slightly. Layer salmon, zucchini mixture and cheese in bottom of pie shell. Beat eggs in medium bowl. Gradually beat in half and half, reserved salmon liquid and seasonings. Pour into shell. Bake until set, about 40 minutes. Cool slightly before slicing into wedges.

❦

Alsatian Apple and Chicken Tart

8 to 10 servings

Hazelnut Pastry
3 cups unbleached all purpose flour
¹/₂ cup finely ground
  toasted hazelnuts
3 tablespoons sugar
1 teaspoon salt
¹/₄ teaspoon freshly grated nutmeg
1 cup (2 sticks) chilled unsalted
  butter, cut into small pieces
3 egg yolks
1 to 2 tablespoons ice water
  (optional)

Dijon mustard

Filling
1¹/₂ cups unsweetened apple cider
1 bay leaf
¹/₂ teaspoon salt
3 lemon slices
3 whole peppercorns
12 ounces skinned and boned
  chicken breasts

1 pound tart green apples
  (such as pippin or Granny
  Smith), peeled, cored and cut
  into ¹/₄-inch-thick slices

3 tablespoons unsalted butter
¹/₄ cup minced shallot
1 medium garlic clove, minced
6 ounces mushrooms, thinly sliced
2¹/₂ teaspoons minced fresh tarragon
3 tablespoons brandy
  Freshly ground white pepper

12 ounces Gruyère cheese, cut into
  ¹/₄-inch cubes
4 eggs, beaten to blend
1 cup whipping cream
1 teaspoon salt
¹/₄ teaspoon freshly grated nutmeg
3 tablespoons chilled unsalted
  butter, cut into small pieces

For pastry: Combine flour, nuts, sugar, salt and nutmeg in large bowl. Cut in butter until coarse meal forms. Mix in yolks and enough water to bind dough. Gather into ball; flatten into disc. Wrap in waxed paper and refrigerate several hours or overnight.

Roll dough out on lightly floured surface to ¹/₄-inch-thick round. Transfer to 11-inch tart pan with removable bottom. Trim and flute edges. Gather scraps and roll out on lightly floured surface to thickness of ¹/₄ inch. Cut out apple design. Transfer to cake pan. Chill crust and apple design 1 hour.

Preheat oven to 425°F. Bake apple design until golden brown, about 6 minutes. Set aside. Line crust with buttered parchment or foil; fill with pie weights or dried beans. Bake crust until set, about 15 minutes. Remove beans and paper. Continue baking until pastry is brown, covering edges with foil if browning too quickly, about 16 to 18 minutes. Cool 10 minutes. Brush crust with Dijon mustard.

For filling: Bring cider, bay leaf, ¹/₂ teaspoon salt, lemon and peppercorns to boil in small saucepan. Add chicken; cover and adjust heat so liquid barely shimmers. Cook until chicken is just springy to touch, about 8 minutes. Drain chicken thoroughly. Cut chicken into ¹/₂ × 2-inch strips. Pat dry.

Place apples in medium saucepan. Add enough water to just cover. Simmer until apples begin to soften, 5 to 6 minutes. Drain well.

Melt 3 tablespoons butter in heavy large skillet over medium heat. Add shallot and garlic. Cook until soft, stirring occasionally, about 3 minutes. Increase heat to medium-high. Add mushrooms and stir until juices evaporate, about 5 minutes. Mix in tarragon. Add brandy and boil until evaporated, about 2 minutes. Season with white pepper. Cool completely.

Combine chicken, mushroom mixture and apples. Spoon into crust. Press cheese into filling. Whisk eggs, cream, 1 teaspoon salt and nutmeg in medium bowl. Gently pour over filling. Dot with 3 tablespoons chilled butter. Bake until filling puffs slightly in center, covering edges with foil if browning too quickly, 35 to 45 minutes. Cool slightly on rack. Top tart with apple design and serve.

Cock-a-Leekie Pie

2 servings

2 chicken legs and thighs
3 cups water
½ onion
1 carrot
1 celery stalk
  Bouquet garni (2 parsley sprigs,
  1 whole clove, ½ bay leaf and
  pinch of dried thyme)
  Pinch of salt

3 tablespoons butter
4 ounces mushrooms, sliced

3 leeks (white part only), trimmed
  and sliced
2 ounces cooked ham, chopped
1 tablespoon minced fresh parsley

Velouté Sauce
2 tablespoons (¼ stick) butter
3 tablespoons all purpose flour
  Salt and freshly ground pepper

Basic Pastry Crust (see page 29)

Combine chicken and water in large saucepan. Bring to boil over high heat, skimming foam as it accumulates on surface. Reduce heat to low. Add onion, carrot, celery, bouquet garni and salt. Cover and simmer until chicken is tender, about 30 to 40 minutes. Remove chicken from pan, reserving stock. When chicken is cool enough to handle, shred meat into bite-size pieces and set aside in large bowl. Strain stock into large saucepan and cook over high heat until reduced to 2 cups, about 15 minutes. Set aside.

Melt 2 tablespoons butter in large skillet over high heat. Add mushrooms and sauté until tender, about 3 to 5 minutes. Add to chicken. Melt remaining 1 tablespoon butter in same skillet. Add leek and sauté until soft. Add to chicken with ham and parsley and toss lightly.

For velouté sauce: Melt butter in heavy medium saucepan over low heat. Add flour and cook, stirring, until mixture is smooth and pale gold. Whisk in reduced chicken stock and simmer, stirring frequently, until mixture is thickened and shiny, about 15 minutes.

Season sauce to taste with salt and pepper. Combine with chicken mixture. Refrigerate overnight before using.

Assemble and bake according to directions with Basic Pastry Crust.

Quail Pies

A delicious adaptation of the game pies sold in delicatessens in Helsinki.

4 servings

Yeast Butter Pastry
1 envelope dry yeast
1 tablespoon sugar
¼ cup warm water (105°F to 115°F)
3 cups all purpose flour
1 teaspoon salt
3 eggs, room temperature
½ cup (1 stick) unsalted butter,
  room temperature

Game Filling
8 bacon strips
4 quail or 2 Cornish game hens
2 cups beef stock
⅓ cup Sherry
1 tablespoon juniper
  berries, crushed
1 garlic clove, minced

2 cups diced peeled
  boiling potatoes
1 cup diced peeled carrots
2 green onions, thinly sliced
½ cup whipping cream
¼ cup minced fresh parsley
1 teaspoon salt
½ teaspoon freshly ground pepper
⅛ teaspoon dried sage, crumbled

1 egg beaten with 2 tablespoons
  milk (glaze)

For pastry: Sprinkle yeast and sugar over warm water. Let stand until yeast bubbles, about 5 minutes. Combine flour and salt in large bowl. Stir in eggs to make stiff dough. Work in butter. Blend in yeast mixture. Slap dough against side of bowl until smooth and elastic, about 50 times. Cover with cloth. Let rise in warm draft-free area until doubled in volume, about 3 hours.

For filling: Wrap 2 bacon strips around each quail. Arrange quail in heavy Dutch oven. Set over medium heat and cook until bacon is browned, about 10 minutes. Add beef stock, Sherry, juniper berries and garlic. Cover and simmer until quail are cooked through, about 45 minutes. Let cool. Remove meat from bones; discard skin and bones. Shred meat and bacon. Set aside in large bowl.

Skim fat from cooking liquid. Boil until liquid is reduced to 1 cup. Add potatoes and carrots. Reduce heat and simmer until vegetables are tender and liquid has almost completely evaporated, about 10 minutes. Add green onions and cook until tender, about 2 minutes. Add to quail mixture. Stir in cream, parsley, salt, pepper and sage.

To assemble: Preheat oven to 375°F. Line baking sheet with parchment paper. Punch dough down. Divide into 4 pieces. Roll each piece out on lightly floured surface into 9-inch circle. Mound ¼ of filling in center of each circle. Bring up sides to enclose filling completely, forming rounds. Set rounds seam side down on prepared sheet. Squeeze gently to eliminate air pockets and to form more perfect round. Brush with glaze. Using scissors, snip air hole in center of each round. Bake until pies are golden, 25 to 30 minutes. Serve immediately.

Turkey Breast Wellington

A superb dinner party entrée. An unusual blend of seasonings enhances the flavor of the turkey, which can be cooked either in the microwave or in a conventional oven.

6 to 8 servings

Yeast Butter Pastry
- 1 envelope dry yeast
- 1 tablespoon sugar
- ¼ cup warm water (105°F to 115°F)
- 3 cups all purpose flour
- 1 teaspoon salt
- 3 eggs, room temperature
- ½ cup (1 stick) unsalted butter, room temperature

Mushroom Pâté
- 3 tablespoons unsalted butter
- 1 pound mushrooms, minced, squeezed dry
- ¼ cup minced green onion
- 1½ tablespoons all purpose flour
- ¼ cup dry Sherry or Madeira
- ½ cup liver pâté
- 1 egg yolk
- ½ teaspoon dried tarragon, crumbled
  Salt and freshly ground white pepper

Turkey
- ½ tablespoon aniseed
- ½ tablespoon rosemary
- ½ tablespoon sage
- ½ tablespoon curry powder
- ½ teaspoon salt
- ¼ teaspoon freshly ground white pepper
- ¼ teaspoon freshly grated nutmeg
- 1 2½- to 3-pound turkey breast, skinned and boned
- 2 tablespoons (¼ stick) unsalted butter
- 1 egg beaten with 2 tablespoons milk (glaze)

For pastry: Sprinkle yeast and sugar over warm water. Let stand until yeast bubbles, about 5 minutes. Combine flour and salt in large bowl. Stir in eggs to make stiff dough. Work in butter. Blend in yeast mixture. Slap dough against sides of bowl until smooth and elastic, about 50 times. Cover and let rise in warm draft-free area until doubled in volume, about 3 hours.

For pâté: Melt butter in heavy large skillet over medium-high heat. Add mushrooms and onion and stir until mushrooms are browned and onion is soft, about 5 minutes. Reduce heat to low, add flour and stir 3 minutes. Pour in Sherry and continue stirring until mixture thickens. Remove from heat. Mix in pâté, yolk and tarragon. Season with salt and pepper. Let cool.

For turkey: Crush aniseed, rosemary and sage in mortar with pestle. Blend in curry powder, salt, pepper and nutmeg. Rub mixture evenly over turkey. Melt butter in heavy large skillet over medium heat. Add turkey and brown on all sides. Place turkey on microwave roasting rack and cook on Medium (or 50 percent power) until instant-reading thermometer registers 135°F. (Or, wrap turkey in foil and roast in 400°F oven until thermometer registers 135°F.) Let cool for 30 minutes.

To assemble: Preheat oven to 375°F. Line baking sheet with parchment paper. Punch dough down. Roll dough out on lightly floured surface into 16-inch square. Spread half of pâté into 4 × 6-inch rectangle in center. Top with turkey, rounded side down. Spread with remaining pâté, covering turkey completely. Lift pastry ends and side, enclosing turkey completely. Set seam side down on prepared sheet. Squeeze gently to eliminate air pockets. Brush with egg glaze. Roll dough scraps out on lightly floured surface. Cut out decorations and arrange over pastry. Brush with egg glaze to secure. Using scissors, snip air hole between decorations. Bake until pastry is golden, about 40 minutes. Serve at room temperature or chilled.

Rabbit Pie

If you bone your own rabbits, save the bones to make a stock for this dish.

4 to 6 servings

1½ pounds boned rabbit (about 3⅓ pounds before boning), cut into 1-inch pieces

All purpose flour seasoned with salt and freshly ground pepper
½ teaspoon minced fresh sage or ¼ teaspoon dried, crumbled
1 teaspoon minced fresh parsley
1 large onion, finely chopped

12 ounces salt pork or side pork, diced
1½ cups (about) rabbit, veal or chicken stock
12 ounces Rough Puff Pastry*
2 tablespoons milk

Soak rabbit in water to cover 1 hour.

Preheat oven to 375°F. Drain rabbit thoroughly and pat dry. Coat evenly with seasoned flour, shaking off excess. Place two inverted custard or egg cups in center of 2½-quart, 3-inch-deep oval casserole or rectangular baking dish. Arrange rabbit in casserole. Sprinkle with sage, parsley and onion. Top with salt pork. Add enough stock to come ¾ way up ingredients.

Roll puff pastry out on lightly floured surface into ¼-inch-thick rectangle slightly longer and wider than casserole. Cover pie with dough; trim and flute edges. Reroll scraps, cut out decorations and affix to top of pie with water. Brush lightly with milk. Cut several 1-inch slits in top of pie to allow steam to escape. Bake until pastry is golden brown, about 30 minutes. Reduce oven temperature to 300°F and continue baking for 1 hour. Serve hot or at room temperature.

*Rough Puff Pastry

Makes 1¼ pounds

6 tablespoons (¾ stick) butter, room temperature
7 tablespoons solid vegetable shortening, room temperature

2 cups all purpose flour
1 teaspoon salt
½ cup plus 2 tablespoons ice water
½ teaspoon fresh lemon juice

Blend butter and shortening thoroughly. Refrigerate until firm. Combine flour and salt in large bowl. Divide butter mixture into fourths. Wrap 3 individually and refrigerate. Cut remainder into flour until mixture resembles coarse meal. Quickly blend in water and lemon juice. Gather dough into ball. Wrap in plastic and refrigerate 30 minutes.

Roll dough out on generously floured surface into 6 × 18-inch rectangle ¼ inch thick. Cut another portion of butter into 1-inch pieces. Press pieces over top ⅔ of rectangle. Fold dough over into 3 equal sections as for business letter. Press edges down lightly with rolling pin to seal. Wrap dough in plastic and refrigerate 15 minutes.

Cut third portion of butter into 1-inch pieces. Turn dough toward you so it opens like a book. Roll dough out on generously floured surface into 6 × 18-inch rectangle. Sprinkle ⅔ with butter. Repeat folding and sealing. Wrap in plastic and refrigerate 15 minutes.

Repeat turning, rolling, folding and sealing with remaining butter. (If at any time dough contracts and is hard to roll, refrigerate 30 minutes.) Wrap in plastic and refrigerate at least 1 hour. (*Can be prepared ahead and refrigerated 3 days or frozen 4 months. Thaw overnight in refrigerator before using.*)

Iron Miner's Pasties

A special sweet-and-savory treat that is traditional in Minnesota. Each pasty is filled with beef and vegetables in one end and spiced apples in the other—a whole meal in one pie.

Makes 8

Country-style Pastry
1¼ cups boiling water
1 cup solid vegetable shortening or lard
1 teaspoon salt
4½ to 5 cups all purpose flour

Beef-Vegetable Filling
1 pound top round of beef, cut into ½-inch pieces
4 cups diced potatoes
1 cup diced carrot
1 large onion, chopped
1 teaspoon salt
½ teaspoon freshly ground pepper

Apple Filling
2 tablespoons sugar
2 teaspoons all purpose flour
½ teaspoon cinnamon
⅛ teaspoon salt
4 medium-size tart green apples, peeled and cut into 12 wedges each

For pastry: Combine water, shortening and salt in large bowl and stir until shortening melts. Add flour and stir until stiff dough forms. Gather into ball. Wrap in plastic and chill 1 hour.

Divide dough into 8 pieces. (Reserve small piece of dough to cut out decorations if desired.) Roll each piece out on floured surface into 9 × 10-inch oval.

For beef-vegetable filling: Combine all ingredients in large bowl.

For apple filling: Mix sugar, flour, cinnamon and salt in large bowl. Add apple slices and toss to coat thoroughly.

To assemble: Preheat oven to 350°F. Line baking sheet with parchment paper. Place 1 cup beef filling in center of each oval. Spread evenly, leaving 2- to 2½-inch border along both sides of filling and enough room at one end to fit length of apple slice. Mound 6 apple slices at empty end. Brush border with water. Gently lift dough border up to enclose filling. Pinch ½-inch lengthwise seam, standing upright. Flute seam. Place toothpick at apple portion. (Or, cut out decorations and affix with water to apple portion.) Repeat with remaining ovals. Arrange on prepared sheet. Bake until golden, about 1 hour. Serve warm.

Lamb and Onion Pirog

An unusual crust and a tangy horseradish sauce enliven this hearty Russian pie.

6 to 8 servings

Lamb and Onion Filling
- 3 tablespoons unsalted butter
- 2 pounds onions, thinly sliced
- 2 tablespoons all purpose flour
- 1 tablespoon dried dillweed
- ½ cup sour cream,
  room temperature

- 1½ pounds ground lamb
- 1 teaspoon salt
  Freshly ground pepper

Caraway-Rye Crust
- 1 envelope dry yeast
- 1 tablespoon firmly packed dark
  brown sugar

- 1 teaspoon salt
- ½ cup warm water (105°F to 115°F)
- ½ cup (1 stick) unsalted butter,
  room temperature
- 3 eggs
- 1 tablespoon caraway seeds
- 1 cup rye flour
- 2 to 2½ cups all purpose flour

- 1 egg beaten with 2 tablespoons
  water (glaze)
  Horseradish Sauce*

For filling: Melt butter in heavy large skillet over low heat. Add onions, cover and cook until onions are soft, stirring occasionally, about 20 minutes. Increase heat to medium, uncover skillet and stir until all liquid evaporates, about 5 minutes. Blend in flour and dill and cook 3 minutes. Stir in sour cream. Transfer to large bowl to cool.

Add lamb to same skillet and cook over high heat, crumbling meat with fork until no pink remains, about 3 minutes. Transfer lamb to onion mixture. Season with salt and pepper. Refrigerate until ready to use. (*Can be prepared 1 day ahead to this point.*)

For crust: Sprinkle yeast, brown sugar and salt into water in bowl. Let stand until yeast bubbles, about 5 minutes. Mix in butter, eggs and caraway seeds. Beat in rye flour. Blend in enough all purpose flour to make stiff dough. Turn dough out onto lightly floured surface and knead until smooth and elastic, about 10 minutes. Wash, dry and oil bowl. Add dough, turning to coat entire surface. Cover with cloth. Let rise in warm draft-free area until doubled, about 1 hour.

Preheat oven to 350°F. Turn dough out onto lightly oiled surface. Knead to expel air bubbles. Reserve ½ cup of dough. Roll remaining dough out into 10 × 18-inch rectangle. Slip large sheet of parchment paper under half of dough. Spoon filling over half on paper, leaving 1½-inch border on 3 outside edges. Fold empty dough over filling. Pinch edges firmly to seal. Slide pirog with parchment onto baking sheet. Brush with glaze. Roll reserved dough out into 4 × 12-inch rectangle. Cut into ½-inch strips. Arrange strips on top, spacing evenly. Prick with fork between strips. Brush with egg glaze. Bake until golden, about 50 minutes. Serve with horseradish sauce.

*Horseradish Sauce

- ½ cup sour cream
- 2 tablespoons grated horseradish
  Salt

Mix sour cream, horseradish and salt to taste in small bowl.

Pork and Apple Pie

2 servings

2 to 3 tablespoons vegetable oil
12 ounces pork (trimmed of fat), cut into ¾-inch cubes
1 medium onion, sliced
1 carrot, sliced
1 tart apple, peeled, cored and sliced
½ cup hard cider

½ cup unsweetened apple juice
½ teaspoon dried sage, crumbled
Salt and freshly ground pepper
¾ cup whipping cream

Basic Pastry Crust
(see following recipe)

Heat oil in large skillet over medium-high heat. Add pork and brown on all sides. Remove from pan. Add onion and carrot to pan and sauté just until onion is limp and golden, about 8 minutes, stirring frequently. Return pork to pan. Blend in apple, hard cider, apple juice, sage, salt and pepper. Reduce heat to low and simmer until meat is tender, 1½ to 2 hours. Stir in cream. Increase heat to high and cook until sauce is syrupy. Remove from heat and let cool. Refrigerate overnight before using.

Assemble and bake according to directions with Basic Pastry Crust.

Basic Pastry Crust

For the flakiest pastry crust use the minimum amount of water.

2 servings

1 cup all purpose flour or ½ cup each all purpose and whole wheat flours
½ teaspoon salt
One of the following (optional):
½ teaspoon celery, fennel or poppy seeds
¼ cup grated sharp cheddar cheese (especially good with Pork and Apple Pie)
2 teaspoons toasted sesame seeds
1 teaspoon grated lemon peel

¼ cup lard
¼ cup (½ stick) chilled butter or margarine
2 to 3 tablespoons ice water

Filling for Cock-a-Leekie Pie (page 24) or Pork and Apple Pie (see previous recipe), well chilled

1 egg yolk beaten with 1 tablespoon water (glaze)

Mix flour and salt in large bowl. Add optional flavoring if desired.

Cut lard and butter into flour mixture using pastry blender or 2 knives until mixture resembles coarse meal. Sprinkle in water a little at a time, mixing until dough begins to cling together. Wrap dough tightly in plastic and refrigerate at least 1 hour or overnight.

Roll chilled pastry out between sheets of waxed paper. Cut into 2 circles slightly larger in diameter than two 1½-cup ramekins or soufflé dishes. Brush rims of dishes and edges of pastry circles with cold water. Divide filling between dishes (filling must be well chilled or underside of pastry will be soggy). Drape pastry over dishes, crimping to seal and trimming any excess. Cut small hole in center of each crust to allow steam to escape.

Preheat oven to 450°F. For final professional touch, use excess pastry to decorate tops of pies with roses, tassels or leaves. Roll scraps out between sheets of waxed paper.

To make rose: Cut ½ × 4-inch strip of dough. Wind strip around itself, starting with tightly wrapped center and making spiral looser as you wind. Open up outside "petals." Cut thin strand of pastry to make stem.

To make tassel: Cut 1 × 3-inch strip of dough. Make cuts across ⅔ of width of strip to form fringe. Roll up lengthwise, pinching base together and opening fringed end of tassel.

To make leaf: Use small scrap of dough and trace leaf or freehand imitation, making veins with small sharp knife. Several leaves can be arranged around hole in crust to form pretty design.

Brush pastry with egg yolk mixture. Bake pies 10 minutes. Reduce oven temperature to 375°F and continue baking until pastry is golden brown, 15 to 20 minutes. Serve immediately.

French-Canadian Meat Pie (Tourtière)

Serve this hearty Canadian favorite for a one-dish winter dinner.

6 to 8 servings

Cheddar Crust
1½ cups all purpose flour
⅓ cup grated aged cheddar cheese
½ teaspoon salt
¼ cup (½ stick) chilled unsalted butter, cut into pieces
¼ cup lard or solid vegetable shortening
¼ cup (or more) ice water

Filling
3 tablespoons vegetable oil
2 medium onions, minced
2 medium garlic cloves, minced
1½ pounds lean ground pork
2 medium tomatoes, peeled, seeded and finely chopped
¼ cup water
½ teaspoon cinnamon
½ teaspoon dried savory, crumbled
¼ teaspoon celery seeds
⅛ teaspoon ground cloves
½ cup fresh breadcrumbs
Salt and freshly ground pepper

1 tablespoon Dijon mustard
1 egg beaten with 2 tablespoons whipping cream (glaze)

For crust: Combine flour, cheese and salt in large bowl. Cut in butter and lard until mixture resembles coarse meal. Blend in ¼ cup ice water just until dough holds together, adding more water if necessary. Divide dough in half. Shape into balls. Wrap in plastic. Chill while preparing filling.

For filling: Heat oil in heavy large skillet over medium-low heat. Add onions and garlic. Cover and cook until translucent, about 10 minutes, stirring occasionally. Add pork and cook until no longer pink, mashing frequently with fork. Mix in tomatoes, water, cinnamon, savory, celery seed and cloves. Reduce heat to medium-low and simmer until most of liquid is absorbed, about 30 minutes. Stir in breadcrumbs, salt and pepper; cool.

Roll 1 portion of dough out on lightly floured surface into ⅛-inch-thick round. Gather dough up on rolling pin and unroll into 10-inch deep-dish metal pie pan. Brush bottom with mustard. Spoon filling into crust. Roll remaining dough out on lightly floured surface into ⅛-inch-thick round. Drape pastry over dish, crimping edges to seal and trimming excess. Reroll dough scraps and cut out leaf shapes. Cut 8 vents in decorative flower petal pattern in top crust to allow steam to escape. Brush pastry with glaze. Arrange pastry leaves atop crust and brush with glaze. (*Can be prepared 1 day ahead. Cover and refrigerate.*)

Preheat oven to 425°F. Bake pie 10 minutes. Reduce oven temperature to 350°F and continue baking until golden brown, about 35 minutes. (If top browns too quickly, drape loosely with aluminum foil.) Serve tourtière hot, warm or at room temperature.

Tourte de la Vallée de Munster

An unusual and delicious meat pie.

6 to 8 servings

2 large shallots, minced
2 tablespoons dry white wine
2 tablespoons Cognac
1 teaspoon salt
¼ teaspoon freshly ground pepper
1 pound pork loin, cut into 2½ × ⅜-inch julienne
1 pound veal top round, cut into 2½ × ⅜-inch julienne

2 pounds puff pastry*

2 tablespoons minced fresh parsley

1 egg yolk, beaten with ¼ teaspoon water (glaze)

1 cup whipping cream, room temperature
2 extra-large eggs, room temperature

Combine shallots, wine, Cognac, salt and pepper in medium bowl. Mix in pork and veal. Refrigerate overnight, stirring occasionally.

Preheat oven to 350°F. Generously butter baking sheet and 9-inch tart ring, or 9-inch tart pan with removable rim. Set tart ring on prepared sheet. Roll half of pastry out on lightly floured surface to ⅛-inch-thick round. Trim to 13-inch circle, reserving trimmings. Fit into tart ring, allowing extra to overhang edges.

Thoroughly drain meats and combine with parsley. Spoon lightly into pastry shell, leaving ¾-inch border around bottom inside edge and mounding slightly in center; do not pack tightly. Fold overhanging dough over edge of filling, pleating at 1½-inch intervals.

Roll remaining pastry out on lightly floured surface to ⅛-inch-thick round. Trim to 11-inch circle, reserving trimmings. Brush pleated edge of bottom pastry layer with glaze. Arrange pastry circle atop tourte, tucking edges down outside of bottom layer, using blunt knife as aid. Press pastry together to seal well.

Stack reserved pastry and roll out to thickness of ⅛ inch. Cut out 3-inch circle using fluted cutter. Brush glaze to 3-inch circle in center of pie. Top with 3-inch pastry circle. Cut ¾-inch hole through pastry circle and top crust. Roll 6 × 4-inch sheet of parchment into cone and fit into hole in pastry. Gently press pastry against cone to seal. Brush tourte with glaze. Very lightly score top with crescent shapes from cone to outer edge.

Bake tourte until golden brown, about 55 minutes. Whisk cream, 2 eggs and pinch of salt to froth. Carefully pour through cone into pie. Remove cone. Bake pie 20 minutes longer. Let cool 20 minutes. Remove any juices atop custard in center of pie with bulb baster just before serving.

*If using packaged frozen pastry, use two 17¼-ounce packages. Stack the 2 sheets in each package and roll out as above.

Ham Piirakka

6 to 8 servings

Flaky Egg Pastry
1²/₃ cups all purpose flour
¼ teaspoon salt
½ cup (1 stick) chilled unsalted
   butter, cut into small pieces
⅓ cup sour cream
1 egg
1 tablespoon fresh lemon juice

Mushroom Pâté
¼ cup (½ stick) butter
12 ounces mushrooms, chopped
½ cup minced white onion
1 8-ounce package cream cheese,
   room temperature
   Salt and freshly ground pepper

1 cup finely chopped walnuts
2 tablespoons brandy

Ham Filling
3 cups ground ham
   (about 1½ pounds)
½ cup coarse breadcrumbs
½ cup snipped fresh chives or
   sliced green onion tops
¼ cup minced fresh parsley
2 eggs, beaten to blend

1 egg beaten with 2 tablespoons
   milk (glaze)
   Sour cream (optional)

For pastry: Combine flour and salt in large bowl. Cut in butter until mixture resembles coarse meal. Beat sour cream, egg and lemon juice to blend. Stir into flour with fork until stiff dough forms. Gather into ball. Wrap in plastic and refrigerate 30 minutes.

For mushroom pâté: Melt butter in heavy large skillet over medium heat. Add mushrooms and onion and cook until all liquid evaporates, stirring occasionally, about 15 minutes; cool. Blend in cream cheese. Add salt and pepper. Stir in walnuts and brandy.

For ham filling: Combine all ingredients.

To assemble: Preheat oven to 400°F. Line baking sheet with parchment paper. Divide dough in half. Wrap 1 portion in plastic and refrigerate to keep from drying. Roll remaining portion out on lightly floured surface into 6 × 12-inch rectangle. Set on prepared sheet. Layer with half of mushroom pâté, half of ham filling, remaining pâté and remaining filling, leaving 1-inch border on all sides. Press filling into rounded log shape. Bring dough edges up sides of filling to make small edge. Roll remaining dough out on lightly floured surface into rectangle slightly larger than first. Make several ½ × 4-inch crosswise slashes in dough. Brush with egg glaze. Set atop filling. Brush edge with egg glaze and crimp to seal. Bake until golden, about 30 minutes. Serve hot, warm or at room temperature. Pass sour cream separately if desired.

Puffy Cheese and Sausage Quiche

6 to 8 servings

Pastry
1⅓ cups all purpose flour
½ teaspoon salt
½ cup (1 stick) chilled unsalted
   butter, cut into ½-inch pieces
2 to 3 tablespoons chilled
   white wine
1 egg yolk

Cheese and Sausage Filling
2 tablespoons vegetable oil
8 ounces lean sausage meat
1 large shallot, minced

7 egg whites
3 eggs
1 cup half and half
½ cup (2¼ ounces) grated
   Monterey Jack cheese
½ cup (2¼ ounces) grated sharp
   cheddar cheese
1 teaspoon baking powder
1 teaspoon salt
½ teaspoon freshly ground
   white pepper

For pastry: Sift flour and salt into large bowl. Cut in butter until mixture resembles coarse meal. Combine wine and egg yolk in small bowl. Add to flour mixture, stirring with fork until moistened. Gather dough into ball. Flatten into 8-inch disc. Wrap in plastic. Refrigerate at least 30 minutes.

Preheat oven to 400°F. Roll dough out on lightly floured surface into 13-inch circle. Roll dough up on rolling pin. Unroll and fit into 10-inch quiche pan, trimming excess and fluting edges. Prick bottom and sides of pastry with fork. Cover dough completely with buttered aluminum foil or waxed paper. Fill with rice, dried beans or pie weights. Bake until set, about 10 minutes. (If edges begin browning too quickly, cover with aluminum foil.) Remove weights and foil or paper. Reduce oven temperature to 375°F and continue baking until lightly browned, about 5 more minutes. Let cool while preparing cheese and sausage filling.

For filling: Preheat oven to 425°F. Heat oil in large skillet over medium heat. Add sausage and shallot and sauté until sausage is cooked through, about 10 to 15 minutes. Discard excess oil. Set mixture aside.

Whisk egg whites in large bowl until frothy. Combine 3 eggs, half and half, cheeses, baking powder, salt and pepper in another bowl. Stir into beaten egg whites. Sprinkle sausage and shallot mixture over bottom of pastry. Pour egg white mixture over sausage. Bake 15 minutes. Reduce oven temperature to 300°F and continue baking until puffed and golden brown, about 40 minutes. Let cool 5 minutes on rack. Cut quiche into wedges and serve.

Tourte of Sausage and Winter Fruits

6 to 8 servings

½ cup water
½ cup sour cream
2 tablespoons (¼ stick) unsalted butter
2 teaspoons sugar
2 teaspoons dry yeast

1 egg
1 teaspoon salt
½ teaspoon freshly ground white pepper
4 cups unbleached all purpose flour (1 pound)

1 12-ounce package mixed dried pitted fruit, finely chopped
1 cup dry white wine

1 tablespoon butter
1 large onion, chopped
2 tablespoons Cognac
2 Granny Smith apples, cored and finely chopped
1 pound kielbasa sausage, cooked, skinned and coarsely chopped
12 ounces Gruyère cheese, shredded
Salt and freshly ground pepper

1 egg beaten with 1 teaspoon cold water (glaze)

Grease large bowl and set aside. Combine water, sour cream, butter and sugar in small saucepan over low heat and warm to 100°F. Remove from heat and let cool to about 60°F. Stir in yeast. Let stand until bubbly, about 10 minutes.

Transfer yeast mixture to processor. Add egg, salt and pepper and mix until blended. Mix in enough flour to make soft, slightly sticky dough. Continue mixing until dough is smooth and elastic. Transfer to prepared bowl, turning to coat entire surface. Cover and let stand at room temperature until more than doubled, about 1½ hours. Punch dough down and let rise again.

Meanwhile, combine mixed fruit and wine in medium bowl and set aside.

Melt butter in large skillet over medium-high heat. Add onion and sauté until browned. Drain wine from fruit and pour into skillet. Increase heat to high, add Cognac and boil, stirring constantly, until reduced to thin glaze. Remove from heat and stir in fruit, apples and sausage. Let cool. Blend in Gruyère. Season with salt and pepper.

Generously grease 11 × 1-inch tart pan with removable bottom. Punch dough down and transfer to lightly floured work surface. Remove ⅔ of dough and roll into 15-inch circle. Press circle into bottom of prepared pan, leaving generous overhang. Spoon fruit filling into pan. Roll out remaining dough as thinly as possible and trim to 13-inch circle (reserve scraps). Moisten edges of both pieces of dough with water. Arrange 13-inch circle over tourte, pinching edges to seal. Fold edges under to form thick coil of dough around tourte. Cut remaining scraps into long, thin strips and decorate top of tourte in crisscross pattern. Cover with towel and let rise until doubled, about 1 hour.

Position rack in bottom third of oven and preheat to 375°F. Brush tourte with beaten egg. Bake until golden brown, about 50 minutes. Cool 20 minutes in pan, then carefully unmold onto wire rack. Serve warm.

Tourte can be prepared 1 day ahead and reheated before serving.

Double Cheese Cornbread Pizza

Makes one 16-inch pizza

Dough
- 1 envelope dry yeast
- ½ cup warm water (105°F to 115°F)

- 1 cup all purpose flour
- 1 cup whole wheat flour
- 1 cup instant masa mix
- 2 teaspoons salt
- 2 tablespoons olive oil
- 1½ cups warm water
- 6 ounces sharp cheddar cheese, grated

Sauce
- 3 tablespoons olive oil
- 2 medium onions, diced
- ½ small carrot, diced

- 2½ pounds tomatoes, peeled
- 1 bouquet garni (thyme, bay leaf, parsley stems)
- 1 tablespoon minced fresh parsley
  Salt and freshly ground pepper

- 12 slices Genoa salami, cut into ½-inch strips
- 1 small head Boston lettuce, cut into ¼-inch strips
- ¼ cup minced cilantro
- 12 ounces Monterey Jack cheese, shredded
- 3 tablespoons corn oil

For dough: Sprinkle yeast over warm water in small bowl and let stand until dissolved; stir to blend. Let stand until slightly foamy, about 10 minutes.

Combine flours, masa mix and salt on work surface. Make well in center. Pour yeast mixture and oil into well. Gradually add water to well, stirring in flour mixture with fork until dough comes together. Turn dough out onto generously floured surface and knead until smooth and elastic, about 10 minutes. Add cheese and knead to combine. Oil large bowl. Add dough, turning to coat entire surface. Cover and let rise in warm draft-free area until doubled in volume, about 1 hour.

For sauce: Heat oil in heavy large saucepan over medium-low heat. Add onions and carrot and cook until soft, stirring occasionally, about 20 minutes. Add tomatoes and bouquet garni and simmer gently until reduced to 3 cups, stirring occasionally, about 1 hour. Add parsley, salt and pepper.

To assemble: Preheat oven to 450°F. Lightly oil 16-inch pizza pan. Spread dough in prepared pan. Spoon sauce over dough, leaving 1-inch border. Arrange salami, lettuce and cilantro atop sauce. Sprinkle with cheese. Drizzle with corn oil. Bake until crust is browned and cheese bubbles, about 40 minutes. (If crust browns too quickly, reduce oven temperature to 425°F.) Let pizza stand for 5 minutes before serving.

3 ❦ Rice and Pasta

The quintessential one-dish meal, a rice- or pasta-based entrée offers the grain itself, a portion of meat or seafood, and vegetables for color and texture. Cooks of many nations prominently feature rice or pasta as "signature" dishes, and some of these international specialties appear here. From Mediterranean lands come Spanish-style Arroz en Cazuela (page 37), One-Hour Paella (page 39), Mixed Grill Couscous (page 40), and Italian pastas. Cajun Quick Baked Jambalaya (page 36) and Special Creole Gumbo (page 37) are streamlined versions of trademark Louisiana dishes, while the spectacular Festive Rice Cake (page 38) provides a taste of Indian cooking.

These stick-to-the-ribs dishes need little in the way of accompaniment. For a family meal or for casual entertaining, a crisp tossed salad would be welcome; dessert might be a cool mousse, custard or *gelato*. Keep in mind, too, that most of the rice mixtures make perfect buffet centerpieces; so do sophisticated baked noodle dishes such as Pasta Vegetable Timbale (page 43) and Gratin of Pasta with Peppers, Tomatoes, Cream and Cheese (page 44). All of these combinations prove yet again that a one-dish meal can be hearty but elegant, easy but impressive.

Kedgeree

6 *servings*

½ cup lentils

1 pound finnan haddie fillets

¾ cup water
1 tablespoon Maggi
liquid seasoning
Pinch of salt

½ cup (1 stick) butter
1 tablespoon curry powder
⅛ teaspoon cayenne pepper
Pinch of crumbled bay leaf
Pinch of dried thyme, crumbled
Pinch of dried dillweed

2 tablespoons finely chopped onion
2 tablespoons finely chopped green
bell pepper
1 cup rice, cooked in chicken stock
until tender
2 hard-cooked eggs, chopped
1 hard-cooked egg, grated
2 tablespoons minced fresh parsley
Paprika

Soak lentils overnight in enough water to cover in heavy medium saucepan.

Simmer finnan haddie in enough water to cover in heavy large skillet until fish flakes easily with fork, about 20 minutes. Drain well. Shred fish, discarding skin and bones.

Add ¾ cup water, Maggi seasoning and salt to undrained lentils and bring to boil. Reduce heat and simmer until lentils are tender, 20 minutes. Drain well, reserving liquid.

Melt butter in heavy large saucepan over medium-low heat. Add curry powder, cayenne pepper, bay leaf, thyme and dillweed and stir 1 minute. Add onion and bell pepper and cook until onion softens slightly, stirring occasionally, 2 to 3 minutes. Mix in lentils, finnan haddie, cooked rice and chopped egg and cook until heated through, stirring occasionally. (If moister texture is desired, add some of reserved lentil liquid.) Spoon onto platter. Garnish with grated egg and minced fresh parsley. Sprinkle with paprika and serve.

Quick Baked Jambalaya

4 *servings*

3 tablespoons vegetable oil
2 large onions, chopped
2 medium-size green bell peppers,
chopped
2 large garlic cloves, crushed
1 28-ounce can tomatoes, drained
and crushed (reserve liquid)
1½ cups cubed cooked ham
½ cup chicken stock or water

1 large bay leaf
1 teaspoon dried thyme, crumbled
½ teaspoon salt
Cayenne pepper

1 pound medium-size raw shrimp,
peeled and deveined
Freshly cooked rice

Preheat oven to 350°F. Heat oil in heavy medium skillet over medium-high heat. Add onions and green peppers and sauté until tender, about 15 minutes. Stir in garlic and cook 3 minutes. Transfer to 9 × 13-inch baking dish. Add tomatoes with liquid, ham, stock, bay leaf, thyme and salt. Season with cayenne. Cover and bake until heated through, about 45 minutes.

Stir shrimp into jambalaya. Cover and bake 5 more minutes. Discard bay leaf. Serve immediately over rice.

Special Creole Gumbo

6 servings

2 tablespoons bacon drippings
2 large celery stalks, diced
1 medium-size green bell pepper, seeded and diced
1 medium garlic clove, minced
2 tablespoons all purpose flour
1 28-ounce can whole tomatoes, undrained
1 14½-ounce can diced okra, drained

1 teaspoon salt
⅛ teaspoon freshly ground pepper

2 cups chopped cooked chicken, uncooked medium shrimp or flaked crabmeat (or mixture of all three)
1 to 2 tablespoons filé powder
Freshly cooked rice

Heat bacon drippings in Dutch oven over medium heat. Add celery, green pepper and garlic and sauté until just tender, about 7 minutes. Blend in flour. Reduce heat to low. Add tomatoes, okra, salt and pepper and simmer 10 minutes.

Stir in chicken and/or seafood and simmer just until chicken is hot or seafood is cooked through, about 2 minutes. Remove from heat and add 1 tablespoon filé powder, adding remaining tablespoon if thicker gumbo is preferred. Continue simmering 5 minutes. Serve hot over freshly cooked rice.

Arroz en Cazuela (Shrimp, Ham and Rice Casserole)

8 servings

¼ cup (½ stick) butter
¼ cup olive oil
4 ounces Italian or garlic sausage, crumbled
2 medium onions, finely chopped
4 garlic cloves, pressed
3 cups chicken stock
3 medium-size ripe tomatoes, minced
4 medium celery stalks, finely chopped
2 medium-size green bell peppers, seeded and cut into strips
2 tablespoons finely chopped fresh parsley

1 tablespoon sugar
1 tablespoon soy sauce
1 teaspoon salt
1 teaspoon turmeric
¼ teaspoon powdered oregano
¼ teaspoon freshly ground pepper
1 bay leaf
2 cups uncooked converted rice
12 ounces frozen tiny shrimp, thawed
8 ounces diced cooked ham

Melt butter with olive oil in Dutch oven over medium heat. Add sausage, onions and garlic and sauté until sausage is browned and onions are soft, about 5 minutes. Stir in remaining ingredients except rice, shrimp and ham. Cook 10 minutes. Add rice. Cover and cook until rice is almost tender, about 10 minutes. Stir in shrimp and ham. Cover and cook until rice is tender and all liquid is absorbed, 8 to 10 minutes. Discard bay leaf and serve.

Festive Rice Cake

Delicious party fare: Layers of shrimp, vegetables and beef alternate with rice for a spectacular presentation.

12 servings

Rice Layer
- 2 cups basmati* or long-grain rice
- 2 tablespoons vegetable oil
- 4 cups water
- 1 teaspoon salt

Shrimp Layer
- 1 pound uncooked fresh medium shrimp, peeled and deveined
- ½ teaspoon Indian chili powder* or cayenne pepper
- ½ teaspoon turmeric
- ½ teaspoon salt

- 6 tablespoons vegetable oil

- 1 large onion, finely chopped
- 6 medium garlic cloves, minced
- 1 large tomato, finely chopped
- 1 teaspoon ground coriander
- ½ teaspoon ground cumin
- 2 tablespoons fresh lemon juice
- 2 tablespoons chopped cilantro

Pea Layer
- 3 cups thawed frozen peas, coarsely mashed
- 2 serrano chilies, finely chopped
- 2 tablespoons vegetable oil
- 1½ teaspoons cumin seeds
- 6 green onions, thinly sliced
- 3 tablespoons fresh lemon juice
- ½ teaspoon salt

Beef Layer
- 5 tablespoons vegetable oil
- 2 medium onions, finely chopped
- ¾ cup finely chopped fresh or canned tomatoes
- 1 pound lean top round of beef, cut into 1-inch cubes
- ½ cup plain yogurt
- 6 medium garlic cloves, minced
- 1 ½-inch piece fresh ginger, peeled and minced
- ¾ teaspoon salt
- 1 tablespoon ground coriander
- 1 teaspoon cumin seeds
- ½ teaspoon Indian chili powder or cayenne pepper
- 6 whole cloves
- 4 cardamom pods, peeled
- 1 2-inch cinnamon stick

- 1 medium-size green bell pepper, sliced into ¼-inch rounds
- 1 medium tomato, sliced into ¼-inch rounds
- Cilantro
- Green onion strips

For rice: Rinse rice under cold water until water runs clear, swirling rice with fingers. Soak rice in cold water to cover 10 minutes. Drain well.

Heat oil in heavy large saucepan over medium-high heat until almost smoking. Add rice and stir 1 minute to coat with oil. Add 4 cups water and salt. Cover and bring to boil. Reduce heat and simmer briskly until water is absorbed, 20 to 25 minutes; do not uncover or stir. Remove from heat and let stand covered 10 minutes. Fluff rice.

For shrimp: Pat shrimp dry. Mix ¼ teaspoon chili powder, ¼ teaspoon turmeric and ¼ teaspoon salt. Rub mixture into shrimp. Let shrimp stand 5 minutes at room temperature.

Heat 3 tablespoons oil in heavy large skillet over medium-high heat until almost smoking. Add shrimp and stir-fry until opaque, about 1 minute per side. Remove from skillet.

Reduce heat to medium. Add onion to same skillet and cook until just tender, stirring frequently, 6 to 8 minutes. Add garlic and cook until onion is golden, stirring frequently, about 5 minutes. Add tomato and remaining salt and cook until tomato liquid evaporates, stirring occasionally, about 10 minutes. Add remaining chili powder, turmeric, coriander and cumin and stir until mixture thickens, about 3 minutes. Blend in shrimp, lemon juice and cilantro.

For peas: Mix peas and chilies. Heat oil in heavy large skillet over medium-high heat until almost smoking. Add cumin seeds and stir until dark, about 1 minute; do not burn. Reduce heat to medium, add green onions and stir 1 minute. Add pea mixture, lemon juice and salt and stir 2 minutes.

For beef: Heat oil in heavy large saucepan over medium-high heat. Add onions and cook until golden brown, stirring frequently, about 12 minutes. Add tomatoes and stir 5 minutes. Add beef, yogurt, garlic, ginger and salt and bring to boil. Reduce heat, cover and simmer until beef is tender and all liquid is absorbed, about 40 minutes. (If no liquid remains and beef is not tender, add ½ cup water and cook covered until done.) Increase heat to high, uncover and cook 7 to 10 minutes to brown beef. Add coriander, cumin, chili powder, cloves, cardamom and cinnamon and cook 5 minutes. Remove cinnamon stick.

To assemble: Preheat oven to 350°F. Line 12-cup flat-bottomed and flat-sided ovenproof glass or metal bowl with foil; oil foil. Arrange bell pepper and tomato slices decoratively on bottom of bowl. Spread with ¾-inch-thick layer of rice. Continue layering with shrimp mixture, ¾-inch-thick layer of rice, pea mixture, ¾-inch-thick layer of rice, meat mixture and remaining rice, pressing firmly between each layer; rice should be level with rim of bowl. Cover tightly with foil and seal around edge. Bake until set and heated through, 25 to 30 minutes. Let cool 5 minutes. Invert bowl onto platter. Carefully remove bowl. Gently remove foil. Garnish with cilantro and green onion and serve.

*Available at Indian markets.

One-Hour Paella

4 servings

4 Italian sausages (about 12 ounces total), cut into 1-inch pieces
1 medium onion, chopped
1 small red bell pepper, chopped
1 small green bell pepper, chopped
2 large garlic cloves, crushed
2 boneless chicken breast halves, skinned and cut into 1-inch pieces

1½ cups long-grain rice
2¼ cups chicken stock
Salt and freshly ground pepper

12 medium prawns in shells
2 medium tomatoes, peeled, quartered and seeded
Pinch of ground saffron
French bread

Sauté sausage in heavy Dutch oven over medium-high heat until cooked through, 5 to 6 minutes. Reduce heat to medium. Add onion, bell peppers and garlic and sauté until onion is soft, about 5 minutes. Add chicken and sauté until lightly browned, 6 to 8 minutes. Add rice and sauté until translucent, about 2 minutes. Add stock, season with salt and pepper and bring to boil. Reduce heat to low, cover and simmer until almost all liquid is absorbed, about 20 minutes.

Stir rice mixture with fork. Add prawns, tomatoes and saffron. Cover and cook until all liquid is absorbed and prawns are pink, 8 to 10 minutes. Serve paella with French bread.

Mixed Grill Couscous

6 to 8 servings

3 tablespoons bacon fat
2 large onions, coarsely chopped
3 celery stalks, sliced ¼ inch thick on diagonal (reserve leaves)
3 10¾-ounce cans chicken broth
1 15½-ounce can garbanzo beans (chickpeas), drained
1 15-ounce can lima beans, undrained
1 7-ounce bottle Pilsner beer
3 carrots, sliced ¼ inch thick on diagonal
4 ounces mushrooms, thinly sliced
1 2-ounce jar chopped pimientos, drained

2 large garlic cloves, minced
2 tablespoons soy sauce
3 bay leaves
1 teaspoon sugar
1 teaspoon poultry seasoning
½ teaspoon freshly ground white pepper

1 1-pound box couscous, cooked according to package directions
3¼ pounds assorted grilled or broiled meats (such as flank steak, filet mignon, kielbasa, lamb chops, pork chops)

Melt bacon fat in Dutch oven over low heat. Add onions and celery and sauté until lightly browned. Add next 13 ingredients. Cover and cook 30 minutes.

Mound couscous in center of large platter. Surround with grilled meats. Ladle vegetables and broth over. Garnish with celery leaves and serve.

Pasta e Fagioli with Ham, Mushrooms and Herbs

One version of the Italian peasant classic. If time permits, you can cook dried cranberry beans or kidney beans to replace the canned.

6 servings

2 tablespoons olive oil
2 medium onions, thickly sliced
2 small carrots, thickly sliced
½ medium-size red bell pepper, cut into thin strips
8 ounces smoked ham, cut into ¼-inch cubes (about 1⅓ cups)
3 tablespoons shredded fresh basil or ½ teaspoon dried, crumbled
4 garlic cloves, minced
Pinch of dried oregano, crumbled
1 15¼-ounce can tomatoes, drained

6 cups chicken stock, degreased
2 1-pound cans kidney beans, drained and rinsed

2½ cups small pasta such as shells or wheels (rotelle)
Salt and freshly ground pepper
¾ cup sliced mushrooms
5 tablespoons shredded fresh basil
⅓ cup sliced green onion tops
Olive oil
Freshly grated Parmesan cheese

Heat 2 tablespoons oil in heavy large saucepan over medium heat. Add onions, carrots and bell pepper. Cook until beginning to soften, stirring occasionally, about 8 minutes. Add ham, 3 tablespoons fresh basil, garlic and oregano. Stir 2 minutes. Add tomatoes. Cook until mixture is reduced to thick sauce, crushing tomatoes with spoon, about 6 minutes. Add stock and beans. Bring to boil, mashing ¼ of beans against sides of pot and skimming surface occasionally. Reduce heat, cover and simmer 15 minutes. (*Can be prepared 1 day ahead.*)

Degrease soup. Bring to boil, stirring occasionally. Add pasta. Boil gently until pasta is almost tender but firm to bite, 6 to 7 minutes. Season with salt and pepper. Sprinkle mushrooms over soup. Remove from heat, cover and let stand 5 minutes. Return soup to boil, stirring constantly. Adjust seasoning. Stir in 5 tablespoons fresh basil. Ladle soup into bowls. Top with green onion and drizzle with oil. Pass Parmesan and freshly ground pepper separately.

Fettuccine with Peas and Ham

4 to 6 servings

5 tablespoons unsalted butter
6 shallots, minced
8 ounces mushrooms, sliced
1¼ cups whipping cream
1 10-ounce package frozen tiny peas, thawed
4 ounces boiled ham, chopped

1 cup freshly grated imported Parmesan cheese
1 pound fettuccine, cooked al dente and drained
Salt and freshly ground pepper
Additional freshly grated Parmesan cheese (optional)

Melt butter in heavy large nonaluminum skillet over medium heat. Add shallots and sauté until soft. Add mushrooms, increase heat to high and cook until mushrooms are very lightly browned. Add cream and boil 2 minutes. Stir in peas and cook about 30 seconds. Reduce heat to low; blend in ham, cheese and fettuccine and toss until heated, well combined and sauce clings to pasta. Season to taste with salt and generous amount of pepper. Turn out onto heated platter and serve. Pass additional cheese if desired.

Sauce can be prepared about 1 hour ahead to point of adding peas.

Fettuccine Milano

6 servings

1 pound spicy Italian sausage meat
½ cup (1 stick) butter
½ cup olive oil
3 cups sliced mushrooms
1 large green bell pepper, seeded and cut into chunks
1 cup minced green onion
1 cup chopped fresh parsley
2 garlic cloves, minced

1 teaspoon dried basil, crumbled
1 teaspoon dried oregano, crumbled
½ teaspoon dried rosemary, crumbled
1 pound fettuccine, cooked al dente and drained
Freshly grated Parmesan cheese

Cook sausage in large skillet over medium-high heat until browned, crumbling with fork, about 10 minutes. Remove with slotted spoon; drain on paper towels. Pour off fat. Melt butter with oil in same skillet. Add mushrooms, bell pepper, green onion, parsley, garlic, basil, oregano and rosemary and sauté until vegetables are tender, about 12 minutes. Remove from heat; stir in sausage. Mound pasta on serving platter. Top with sausage mixture, sprinkle with Parmesan and serve.

Pasta with Tomatoes and Four Cheeses

Perfect for warm summer nights since the sauce requires no cooking.

4 to 6 servings

2¾ pounds tomatoes, cored, seeded and cut into ¾-inch cubes
½ cup shredded fresh basil
1½ teaspoons coarse kosher salt
1 large garlic clove, minced

1 cup ricotta cheese, room temperature
2 tablespoons (about) whipping cream
Freshly ground pepper
Freshly grated nutmeg

2 ounces Fontina cheese, cut into ¼-inch cubes (½ cup)
2 ounces fresh mozzarella cheese, cut into ¼-inch cubes (½ cup)

1 pound rotelle or other short pasta
2 tablespoons olive oil (preferably extra-virgin)
1 cup freshly grated Parmesan cheese

Combine first 4 ingredients in medium bowl. Let stand at room temperature 1 to 2 hours, stirring occasionally.

Fluff ricotta with fork. Thin to creamy consistency with whipping cream. Season with pepper and nutmeg. Mix in Fontina and mozzarella. Let stand at room temperature while cooking pasta.

Drain most of liquid from tomatoes, leaving just enough to keep moist. Add pasta to large amount of rapidly boiling salted water, stirring to prevent sticking. Cook until just tender but still firm to bite. Drain well. Place in heated bowl. Mix in oil. Add cheese mixture and toss until cheese begins to melt. Spoon tomato mixture over top; toss at table. Sprinkle each serving with some of Parmesan. Pass remaining cheese separately.

Fresh Pasta with Goat Cheese and Scallops

The pasta can be freshly made or prepared in advance and dried.

6 to 8 servings

1½ cups all purpose flour
6 extra-large eggs

2 cups whipping cream
4 ounces California goat cheese, cut into small chunks

1 pound bay scallops, patted dry
Salt and freshly ground pepper
¼ cup (½ stick) butter

40 baby asparagus, blanched, trimmed to 4 inches
1 bunch basil, stemmed and cut into julienne (about 1 loosely packed cup)
2 tablespoons snipped fresh chives

Mound flour on work surface or in large bowl and make well in center. Add eggs to well and blend with fork. Gradually draw flour from inner edge of well into center until all flour is incorporated. Gather dough into ball. Wrap in plastic; let stand 30 minutes.

Cut dough into 3 pieces. Flatten 1 piece of dough (keep remainder covered), then fold into thirds. Turn pasta machine to widest setting and run dough through about 10 times until smooth and velvety, folding before each run and dusting with flour if sticky. Adjust machine to next narrower setting. Run dough through machine without folding. Repeat narrowing rollers after each run until pasta is ¹⁄₁₆ inch thick, dusting with flour as necessary. Hang dough sheet on drying rack or place on kitchen towels. Repeat with remaining dough. Dry sheets until leathery and edges just begin to curl. *Pasta must be cut at this point or dough will be too brittle.* Run sheets through thinnest blades of pasta machine to cut. Arrange strands on towel, overlapping as little as possible.

Boil cream with cheese until reduced to 1½ cups. Set aside.

Season scallops with salt and pepper. Melt butter in heavy large skillet over high heat. Add scallops and sauté on both sides until firm, about 1 minute.

Cook pasta in large amount of rapidly boiling salted water until just tender but firm to bite. Drain well. Reheat cream mixture. Set aside 8 scallops, 20 asparagus and 2 tablespoons basil. Stir remaining scallops, asparagus and basil into sauce. Add to pasta and toss well. Season generously with salt and pepper. Mound pasta on plates. Decorate with reserved scallops, asparagus and basil. Sprinkle with chives and serve.

Linguine with New England Clam Sauce

4 servings

1/4 cup (1/2 stick) butter
1 1/2 cups minced onion
1/2 cup diced carrot
1/2 cup diced celery
1/2 cup diced green bell pepper
3 tablespoons all purpose flour
2 cups fish or chicken stock
1/2 cup dry white wine

1/2 teaspoon dried thyme, crumbled
1/4 teaspoon freshly ground pepper
3 dozen littleneck clams, scrubbed

1 pound linguine or spaghetti
1/4 cup (1/2 stick) butter
Salt
1/4 cup minced fresh parsley

Melt 1/4 cup butter in large skillet over medium-low heat. Add vegetables, cover and cook until mixture begins to soften, about 5 minutes. Sprinkle with flour and stir 3 minutes. Mix in stock, wine, thyme and pepper. Boil until sauce thickens, stirring constantly, about 5 minutes. Add clams. Cover and steam 5 minutes. Remove opened clams. Cover and continue cooking remaining clams about 5 minutes longer; discard any that do not open.

Remove 24 clams from shells; return to skillet. Keep sauce warm.

Cook pasta in large pot of boiling salted water until just tender but firm to bite. Drain well. Transfer to large bowl. Mix in 1/4 cup butter.

Season sauce with salt. Pour over pasta. Add parsley and toss to blend. Divide among heated shallow bowls. Garnish with remaining clams (in shells). Serve immediately.

Pasta-Vegetable Timbale (Timballo di Collesano)

A terrific party dish.

8 to 10 servings

3 pounds fennel (tough outer layer discarded), center stalk reserved
2 3/4 pounds broccoli, trimmed, stems peeled
2/3 cup olive oil
1 very large onion, minced
3 3-ounce cans tomato paste
1 1/2 teaspoons (scant) salt
2 2-ounce cans anchovies in oil, well drained

2 tablespoons olive oil
2 cups dry breadcrumbs

1 cup (4 ounces) freshly grated Romano or caciocavallo cheese
1 teaspoon freshly ground pepper

1 1/4 pounds penne or other tubular pasta

Blanched broccoli (garnish)
Freshly grated Romano or caciocavallo cheese

Quarter fennel bulbs lengthwise, then cut into thin wedges. Cut center stalk into 1/4-inch pieces. Cut broccoli florets off stems. Thinly slice stems. Heat 1/3 cup oil in heavy large saucepan over medium-high heat. Add half of onion and stir until it sizzles, about 2 minutes. Add half of tomato paste and stir 2 minutes. Mix in 1 cup water. Add fennel and enough water to cover fennel by 2/3. Add 3/4 teaspoon salt. Cover, reduce heat and simmer until fennel is tender, about 15 minutes. Uncover, increase heat to high and stir until liquid is reduced by half. Transfer to very large pot or bowl. Repeat with broccoli, using 1/3 cup oil, remaining onion, tomato paste and salt. Add broccoli mixture to fennel. Transfer 2 tablespoons liquid to bowl. Add anchovies and mash to combine. (*Can be prepared 4 hours ahead to this point.*)

Preheat oven to 325°F. Heat 2 tablespoons oil in heavy large skillet over medium heat. Add 1 1/3 cups breadcrumbs and stir until golden brown, about

2 minutes. Remove from heat and continue stirring 2 minutes. Add to vegetables. Mix in mashed anchovies, 1 cup cheese and pepper.

Add pasta to large pot of rapidly boiling water, stirring to prevent sticking. Cook until just tender but firm to bite. Drain well. Mix into vegetables.

Brush 10 × 14-inch pan with 3-inch sides with oil. Coat with remaining ⅔ cup breadcrumbs. Transfer vegetable mixture to pan, packing down well. Bake until hot, about 45 minutes. Invert onto platter if desired. Garnish with blanched broccoli. Serve hot, passing cheese separately.

Gratin of Pasta with Peppers, Tomatoes, Cream and Cheese

The Tomato Sauce for this easy dish can be made several days ahead.

4 to 6 servings

1 pound rotelle or other short pasta
1 tablespoon olive oil

2 cups Tomato Sauce*
1 charred and peeled red bell pepper, cut into 1-inch pieces
1 charred and peeled green bell pepper, cut into 1-inch pieces

1⅓ cups whipping cream
1¼ cups freshly grated Parmesan cheese
Additional freshly grated Parmesan cheese
Freshly ground pepper

Add pasta to large pot of rapidly boiling salted water, stirring to prevent sticking. Cook until just tender but still firm to bite. Drain. Rinse with cold water and drain. Toss with oil.

Preheat oven to 400°F. Butter 8-cup oval gratin dish or shallow baking dish. Pour in ½ cup tomato sauce. Cover with ¼ of pasta, ¼ of peppers, ⅓ cup cream and ¼ cup cheese. Repeat 3 times. Sprinkle with ¼ cup Parmesan. Bake until top is browned and bubbly, about 30 minutes. (Run briefly under broiler if browner top is desired.) Serve hot. Pass additional Parmesan and pepper separately.

*Tomato Sauce

Makes about 3 cups

1 tablespoon butter
1 tablespoon olive oil
1 small onion, chopped
2 medium garlic cloves, minced
2 2-pound 3-ounce cans peeled whole Italian plum tomatoes, drained and coarsely chopped
½ teaspoon dried basil, crumbled
½ teaspoon salt

1 bay leaf
Pinch of dried thyme, crumbled
Pinch of sugar (optional)
Freshly ground pepper
⅓ cup shredded fresh basil
3 tablespoons minced fresh parsley

Melt butter with oil in heavy large saucepan over medium heat. Add onion and cook until translucent, stirring occasionally, about 8 minutes. Add garlic and stir 2 minutes. Mix in all remaining ingredients except fresh basil and parsley. Increase heat to medium-high and boil until mixture is thickened, stirring frequently, about 10 to 20 minutes. Discard bay leaf. Taste and adjust seasoning. (*Can be prepared 3 days ahead. Cover and refrigerate. Reheat before using.*) Just before serving, stir in fresh basil and parsley.

4 ❦ Vegetables and Salads

For the last few years vegetables have been getting, to put it mildly, very good press. Replete with vitamins, minerals, fiber and those complex carbohydrates that nutritionists prize, vegetables—either on their own or enriched with a bit of meat or cheese—are moving right to the center of the plate.

Happily, while vegetables are just the thing for the diet-conscious, the splendid one-dish meals in this chapter are far removed from the kinds of "health foods" that have earned themselves such a dubious reputation. Consider Hungarian Mushroom Paprikás (page 48) over homemade noodles . . . tangy Eggplant, Tomato and Kashkaval Gratin with Sesame Seeds (page 47) . . . or luxurious Vegetable Strudel (page 50). Tempted by such robust combinations, would anyone miss a meat entrée?

To complement these hot dishes the chapter is rounded out with an assortment of inventive main-course salads. For a meatless meal choose Marinated Vegetable and Tofu Salad (page 51), Fusilli Salad with Quick Aïoli Dressing, Tricolored Pasta Salad with Mozzarella (both on page 52), or one of the sophisticated seafood mixtures. On the other hand, if you love the rich flavor of cured and smoked meats try the unusual Warm Bernese Onion Salad (page 55) or Ham, Gruyère and Cabbage in Roquefort Dressing (page 56).

Given the current explosion of interest in vegetables—from both nutritional and gastronomic standpoints—there is little doubt that we will be eating a lot more of them in the coming years, particularly as main dishes. Here is the perfect opportunity to start.

❦ *Hot Vegetable Dishes*

Savoy Cabbage in Casserole

4 to 5 servings

5½ cups very coarsely chopped
   Savoy or Napa cabbage
   Salt and freshly ground pepper
2 medium tomatoes, peeled, cored,
   seeded and chopped
2 bacon slices
1 teaspoon butter
1 large onion, coarsely chopped

1 tablespoon butter
1½ tablespoons all purpose flour

⅓ cup milk
¼ teaspoon salt
⅛ teaspoon freshly ground pepper
⅓ cup sour cream, room
   temperature
5 to 6 ounces grated Muenster
   cheese

Spread cabbage in even layer on bottom of 10-inch square baking dish. Season with salt and pepper to taste. Top with tomatoes. Cook bacon in small skillet over medium heat until crisp. Remove with slotted spoon and drain on paper towels. Crumble bacon over tomatoes. Discard all but 1 teaspoon fat from skillet. Add 1 teaspoon butter to skillet, place over medium heat and let melt. Add onion and cook until wilted, 3 to 4 minutes, stirring occasionally. Remove onion from skillet using slotted spoon and arrange evenly in dish. Discard fat in skillet.

Preheat oven to 350°F. Melt 1 tablespoon butter in same skillet over medium-low heat. Gradually add flour, whisking 3 minutes. Gradually blend in milk, stirring until smooth; do not boil. Add salt and pepper. Remove sauce from heat and blend in sour cream. Spoon over cabbage mixture. Sprinkle top with grated cheese. Cover with foil and bake 20 minutes. Remove foil and continue baking until cabbage is tender, about 30 minutes. Cool several minutes before serving.
Can be prepared ahead and reheated.

Corn "Risotto" with Chicken Livers and Mushrooms

2 servings

3 tablespoons unsalted butter
1½ cups fresh corn kernels (about
   2 medium ears)
¼ cup minced onion
½ cup whipping cream
2 tablespoons grated Gruyère
   cheese

2 medium shallots, minced
12 ounces chicken livers, trimmed
   and patted dry

16 okra pods
12 fresh shiitake mushroom caps
2 medium-size red bell peppers,
   cored, seeded and cut into strips
1 teaspoon filé powder
¼ cup chicken stock
   Salt and freshly ground pepper

Melt 1 tablespoon butter in heavy medium skillet over medium heat. Add corn and onion and cook 5 minutes, stirring occasionally. Add cream and simmer until mixture thickens, stirring occasionally, about 10 minutes. Add cheese and stir 1 minute. Transfer to food processor and chop coarsely; mixture should be thick and creamy.

Melt remaining 2 tablespoons butter in heavy medium skillet over medium heat. Add shallots and stir 1 minute. Add chicken livers, okra, mushroom caps and bell peppers and sauté until livers are browned and vegetables are crisp-tender, about 5 minutes. Stir in filé powder. Add stock and cook to reduce slightly. Season with salt and pepper. Spoon corn into center of plate. Alternate bell pepper and okra around corn. Spoon livers and mushrooms over corn. Serve immediately.

Eggplant, Tomato and Kashkaval Gratin with Sesame Seeds

Accompany this entrée with plenty of crusty bread.

2 servings

1 large eggplant, stemmed, peeled and cut crosswise into
³/₈-inch-thick slices
Salt

8 tablespoons (about) olive oil
1 large onion, thinly sliced
¼ teaspoon dried thyme, crumbled
Freshly ground pepper

12 ounces small tomatoes, peeled and cut crosswise into
¼-inch-thick slices

2 cups (about 8 ounces) coarsely grated Kashkaval cheese*
1 tablespoon sesame seeds

Sprinkle both sides of eggplant lightly with salt. Place in colander and top with bowl containing heavy can to weight down. Let drain 1 hour, turning after 30 minutes. Pat dry.

Heat 1 tablespoon oil in heavy medium skillet over low heat. Add onion, thyme, pepper and pinch of salt. Cook, stirring frequently, until very tender, about 20 minutes. Set aside.

Preheat oven to 425°F. Line baking sheet with foil. Arrange tomato slices in single layer on rack. Remove seeds using point of knife. Set rack on prepared sheet. Sprinkle tomatoes lightly with salt. Bake 10 minutes to remove excess juice. Set aside. Reduce oven temperature to 400°F.

Heat 2 tablespoons oil in heavy large skillet over medium heat. Cook eggplant in batches (do not crowd) until just tender when pierced with fork, about 2 minutes on each side, adding 2 tablespoons oil to skillet before cooking each batch. Transfer to large plate. (*Can be prepared 4 hours ahead to this point. Let stand at room temperature.*)

Brush 5-cup gratin dish with olive oil. Arrange half of eggplant in single layer in dish. Sprinkle with pepper. Spread onion over eggplant. Top with ½ cup grated cheese. Arrange remaining eggplant in single layer atop cheese and sprinkle with pepper. Arrange tomatoes in single layer on top. Brush with 2 teaspoons olive oil. Top with remaining cheese and sprinkle with sesame seeds. Bake until cheese begins to brown, about 15 minutes.

Preheat broiler. Broil gratin until topping is golden brown, about 1 minute. Let stand 5 minutes before serving.

*Available at Greek, Eastern European or Middle Eastern markets or specialty cheese shops. Kefalotyri cheese can be substituted, but will not brown as well.

Hungarian Mushroom Paprikás

Serve over homemade noodles.

4 servings

½ cup vegetable oil
3 cups chopped onion
1 large tomato, chopped
1 small green bell pepper, chopped
2 large garlic cloves, minced
1½ cups chicken stock, preferably homemade
2 tablespoons Hungarian sweet paprika

Pinch of sugar
Salt and freshly ground pepper
1 pound mushrooms, chopped
3 tablespoons sour cream, room temperature
Additional sour cream

Heat oil in heavy large deep skillet over medium-low heat. Add onion, tomato, green pepper and garlic and cook, stirring frequently, until onion is tender. Transfer mixture to blender. Add stock and puree until smooth. Return mixture to skillet and stir in paprika, sugar, salt and pepper. Add mushrooms, place over medium-high heat and boil until liquid is reduced to desired consistency. Remove from heat and stir in 3 tablespoons sour cream. Top with additional dollop of sour cream and serve.

Nutburgers

A tasty vegetable-nut patty that is fried, topped with cheese and served in pita bread with avocado, lettuce, tomato and a creamy dressing.

8 servings

3 15-ounce cans garbanzo beans (chickpeas), rinsed, drained and mashed or pureed
1 medium-size red onion, finely chopped
½ bunch parsley, finely chopped
½ cup chopped almonds (2 ounces)
½ cup chopped walnuts (2 ounces)
¼ cup roasted sunflower seeds (1 ounce)
1 teaspoon curry powder
½ teaspoon vegetable salt

1 egg, beaten to blend

Vegetable oil (for frying)
Sharp cheddar cheese slices

8 pita rounds, 1 edge trimmed for filling
Spicy mustard
3 tomatoes, chopped
2 avocados, peeled, pitted and finely diced
½ head green leaf lettuce, chopped
Creamy Herbal Dressing*

Combine beans, onion, parsley, nuts, sunflower seeds, curry powder and vegetable salt in large bowl. Add beaten egg and mix well. Form mixture into eight 3 × ¾-inch patties.

Pour oil into heavy large skillet to depth of ¼ inch. Place over medium-high heat. When oil is hot, add patties (in batches if necessary) and fry until lightly browned on bottom, about 4 minutes. Turn and fry other side until browned, about 4 minutes, topping each patty with slice of cheese while second side cooks. Drain patties on paper towels.

Lightly spread inside of pitas with mustard. Place patty in each. Add tomato, avocado and lettuce. Spoon dressing over filling and serve immediately.

*Creamy Herbal Dressing

Makes about 1 cup

½ cup mayonnaise
½ cup plain yogurt
2 tablespoons finely chopped onion
2 tablespoons finely chopped fresh parsley

¼ teaspoon cider vinegar
¼ teaspoon fresh lemon juice
¼ teaspoon Worcestershire sauce
¼ teaspoon vegetable salt

Combine all ingredients in processor or blender and mix until smooth.

Winter Vegetable Platter with Mustard Sauce

Complement this attractive, warming entrée with chewy black bread.

4 to 6 servings

Mustard Sauce
- ¼ cup (½ stick) butter
- 1½ tablespoons all purpose flour
- ¼ teaspoon salt
  Pinch of cayenne pepper (optional)
- 1 cup half and half
- 1 tablespoon Dijon mustard
- 1 egg yolk, room temperature
- 1 tablespoon dry white wine

Vegetables
- 1 medium kohlrabi, trimmed, peeled and cut into ¼-inch-thick slices
- 1 medium turnip, trimmed, peeled and cut into ¼-inch-thick slices
- 1 small symmetrically shaped rutabaga, trimmed, peeled and cut into ¼-inch-thick slices
- 4 medium carrots, trimmed, halved crosswise and thicker piece halved lengthwise
- 4 to 5 small leeks (white part only), halved lengthwise, rinsed and drained
- 1 medium fennel bulb, trimmed of all but lower 3½ to 3¾ inches of stalk, outer stalks removed and inner stalks cut into ⅝-inch-wide pieces
- 10 to 12 medium cauliflower florets

For sauce: Melt butter in small saucepan over medium-low heat. Gradually stir in flour and cook, stirring constantly, 3 minutes. Blend in salt and cayenne pepper. Gradually add half and half, stirring constantly until mixture thickens and boils. Reduce heat and simmer 1 minute, stirring constantly. Remove from heat. Blend in mustard. Beat yolk and wine in small bowl. Beat ⅓ of mustard mixture into yolks several drops at a time. Stir yolks back into mustard mixture. Place over low heat and cook, stirring constantly, until sauce is hot and thickened slightly, 2 to 3 minutes; *do not boil or sauce will curdle.* Cover and set aside. (*Can be prepared ahead and rewarmed over low heat.*)

For vegetables: Add water to steamer to within 1 inch of rack. Place over high heat and bring to boil. Rinse and drain kohlrabi, turnip and rutabaga. Arrange sliced vegetables in separate bundles on steamer rack. Cover, reduce heat to medium-high and cook 6 minutes. Rinse and drain carrots, leeks and fennel. Arrange carrots over rutabaga, leeks over turnip and fennel over kohlrabi. Cover and cook 8 minutes. Rinse and drain cauliflower florets. Arrange over top of vegetables. Cover and continue steaming until vegetables are tender, 4 to 5 minutes.

To serve, mound cauliflower florets in center of heated large round platter. Surround cauliflower with remaining vegetables, alternating colors. Pour half of mustard sauce over vegetables and serve; pass remaining sauce separately.

Zucchini-Avocado Sauté

6 servings

- ¼ cup (½ stick) butter
- 8 ounces mushrooms, thinly sliced
- 3 zucchini, thinly sliced (about 4 cups)
- 1 green bell pepper, cored, seeded and thinly sliced
- 2 avocados, peeled, pitted and sliced
- 8 ounces Swiss cheese, grated (about 3 cups)
- 1 tablespoon chili powder

Melt butter in large skillet over medium heat. Add mushrooms and sauté until tender, about 5 minutes. Remove from skillet using slotted spoon and set aside. Add zucchini and green pepper to skillet and sauté until crisp-tender, about 10 minutes. Remove from heat. Add avocado and mushrooms. Sprinkle with cheese and chili powder and toss lightly. Transfer sauté to platter and serve immediately.

Vegetarian Chili

6 servings

¼ cup vegetable oil
2 cups chopped onion
3¾ cups chopped tomatoes
3⅔ cups sliced mushrooms
2 cups broccoli florets
2 cups sliced zucchini
1 cup chopped green bell pepper
3 tablespoons chili powder
½ teaspoon garlic powder
⅛ teaspoon freshly ground pepper

¼ cup water
2 teaspoons all purpose flour
2 8¾-ounce cans red kidney beans, drained
3 cups freshly cooked rice
Sour cream
Chopped green onion
Shredded cheddar cheese

Heat oil in Dutch oven over medium-high heat. Add onion and sauté until translucent and slightly softened. Reduce heat to medium and add tomatoes, mushrooms, broccoli, zucchini, bell pepper, chili powder, garlic powder and pepper. Cover and simmer until vegetables are crisp-tender, about 10 minutes. Combine water and flour and stir into vegetable mixture. Add beans and cook until chili thickens, stirring frequently, about 5 minutes. Divide rice among bowls. Spoon chili over rice. Top with sour cream, green onion and cheese. Serve hot.

Vegetable Strudel

6 to 8 servings

3 cups chopped fresh broccoli
3 cups chopped fresh cauliflower
2½ cups chopped carrot

2 tablespoons (¼ stick) butter
1 large onion, coarsely chopped
2 garlic cloves, finely chopped

3 eggs
2 teaspoons minced fresh parsley
1½ teaspoons dried basil, crumbled
1 teaspoon minced fresh tarragon or ½ teaspoon dried, crumbled

1 teaspoon salt
Freshly ground pepper
1 pound Swiss or cheddar cheese, shredded

14 phyllo pastry sheets
6 tablespoons (¾ stick) butter, melted
Sesame seeds (optional)
Hollandaise sauce

Combine broccoli, cauliflower and carrot in steamer. Place over boiling water and steam until crisp-tender. Let cool slightly.

Melt butter in medium skillet over medium heat. Add onion and garlic. Cover and cook, stirring occasionally, until golden, about 10 minutes. Let mixture cool to lukewarm.

Combine eggs, parsley and seasonings in large bowl and beat well. Add steamed vegetables, onion mixture and shredded cheese and mix well.

Preheat oven to 375°F. Oil large baking sheet and set aside. Place 1 phyllo sheet on work surface (cover remaining phyllo with plastic wrap to prevent drying). Brush with melted butter. Stack remaining phyllo sheets on top, brushing all but last sheet with butter. Spread vegetable mixture onto dough, leaving 3-inch border on all sides. Fold in short ends of dough, then fold in long sides, overlapping at center. Brush with butter to seal. Carefully transfer strudel to prepared baking sheet. Brush top with butter. Sprinkle with sesame seeds if desired. Bake until golden, about 20 to 30 minutes. Transfer to heated platter and serve immediately. Accompany with hollandaise sauce.

🥄 *Main-Dish Salads*

Marinated Vegetable and Tofu Salad

6 servings

1 pound bean sprouts
2 cups sliced mushrooms
2 green onions, sliced
1 cup sliced cauliflower
1 English cucumber, sliced
1 carrot, thinly sliced
1 green bell pepper, cored, seeded and cut into strips
1 cup broccoli florets

Sesame Dressing
1 cup white vinegar
½ cup vegetable oil
¼ cup sugar

2 tablespoons oriental sesame oil
1 to 2 tablespoons soy sauce
1 tablespoon sesame seeds
1 large garlic clove, crushed
2 teaspoons grated fresh ginger
    Salt and freshly ground pepper
    Hot chili oil

⅓ cup minced onion
3 tablespoons vegetable oil
¼ teaspoon turmeric
1 pound tofu, cubed or mashed
1½ teaspoons soy sauce
    Salt

Combine first 8 ingredients in large bowl.

For dressing: Mix next 11 ingredients in processor or blender. Pour dressing over vegetables and toss lightly. Refrigerate several hours or overnight.

Just before serving, drain vegetables thoroughly. Combine onion, oil and turmeric in medium skillet over medium heat and stir until hot. Add tofu, soy sauce and salt and stir until heated through. Spoon over vegetables and serve immediately.

Rice Salad with Sausage and Peppers

The next time you are barbecuing, brush some extra bell peppers and onion slices with olive oil and grill them until browned on all sides, then use them in this salad.

4 to 6 servings

1¼ cups long-grain rice
8 ounces (about) grilled Italian sausage, cut into ½-inch cubes
1 to 2 grilled bell peppers, cut into ½-inch cubes
4 to 6 grilled onion slices, cut into ½-inch cubes
½ cup olive oil
¼ cup shredded fresh basil

3 tablespoons fresh lemon juice
2 tablespoons minced fresh parsley
1 teaspoon salt
    Freshly ground pepper
    Sliced radishes
    Oil-cured olives
    Fresh basil leaves

Cook rice in large amount of boiling salted water until just tender but firm to bite, 12 to 13 minutes. Drain. Rinse with warm water; drain well. Transfer rice to large bowl. Mix in sausage, peppers, onions, oil, shredded basil, lemon juice, parsley, salt and pepper. Adjust seasoning. Cool to room temperature. (*Can be prepared 1 day ahead and refrigerated. Bring to room temperature before serving.*) Garnish salad with radishes, olives and basil leaves.

🥄

Fusilli Salad with Quick Aïoli Dressing

8 servings

1 pound freshly cooked fusilli pasta
2 6½-ounce jars marinated artichoke hearts (undrained)
1¼ cups Quick Aïoli Dressing*
¾ cup frozen peas, cooked
¾ teaspoon salt

¼ teaspoon freshly ground pepper
Romaine lettuce leaves
Parsley sprigs
1 lemon, cut into 8 wedges
Sun-dried tomatoes (optional)
Cayenne pepper

Combine fusilli, artichoke hearts with marinade, dressing, peas, salt and pepper and toss well. Line salad bowl with lettuce. Mound fusilli mixture in center. Garnish with parsley sprigs, lemon wedges and sun-dried tomatoes. Sprinkle lightly with cayenne. Serve immediately.

*Quick Aïoli Dressing

Makes 2¼ cups

10 garlic cloves
2 cups mayonnaise

¼ cup fresh lemon juice
1 teaspoon Dijon mustard

Mince garlic finely in processor. Add mayonnaise, lemon juice and mustard and process until smooth, about 15 seconds.

Tricolored Pasta Salad with Mozzarella

4 servings

1 garlic clove, crushed
¼ teaspoon salt
½ cup olive oil
¼ cup red wine vinegar or balsamic vinegar
½ teaspoon dried oregano, crumbled
¼ teaspoon fresh thyme, minced
1 cup freshly cooked tricolored pasta

1 cup cubed mozzarella cheese
1 7½-ounce can baby corn, drained and cut into 1-inch pieces
½ cup carrot julienne, blanched
½ cup cauliflower florets, cooked until crisp-tender
½ cup halved stuffed green olives
Salt and freshly ground pepper

Mash garlic and ¼ teaspoon salt in mortar with pestle. Transfer to small bowl. Add olive oil, vinegar, oregano and thyme and mix well. Combine pasta, cheese, corn, carrot, cauliflower and olives in large bowl. Pour dressing over and toss to mix well. Season with salt and pepper. Serve immediately.

Salade de Lotte et Pâtes Fraîches (Monkfish and Pasta Salad)

The vegetables can be blanched ahead of time and held, covered, at room temperature.

4 servings

5 to 6 ounces green beans, cut into ½-inch pieces
1 medium-size red bell pepper, cut into ¼-inch julienne
1 medium carrot, cut diagonally into paper-thin slices
1 medium zucchini, cut diagonally into paper-thin slices
7 ounces fresh tagliatelle pasta

¼ cup Sherry vinegar
2 teaspoons Dijon mustard

Salt and freshly ground pepper
¾ cup olive oil

Mixed lettuce leaves (such as mâche, oak leaf, endive)
Chervil sprigs

12 ounces skinned and boned monkfish fillets, cut diagonally into ¼-inch-thick slices
2 tablespoons olive oil
1 tablespoon snipped fresh chives

Cook green beans and red pepper separately in boiling salted water until crisp-tender. Rinse under cold water. Drain and pat dry. Set aside.

Combine carrot and cold salted water to cover and bring to boil. Cook until tender. Rinse under cold water. Drain carrot well and pat dry.

Cook zucchini in boiling salted water until tender. Rinse under cold water. Drain well and pat dry.

Cook tagliatelle in boiling salted water until just tender but firm to bite. Rinse under cold water. Drain well.

Blend vinegar, mustard and salt and pepper in large bowl. Whisk in ¾ cup oil in thin stream. Adjust seasoning. Add tagliatelle, blanched green beans and bell pepper and toss well.

Arrange 2 leaves of each kind of lettuce and chervil sprig on chilled plate. Mound pasta in center. Curl carrot and zucchini slices around pasta.

Pat fish dry. Sprinkle with salt and pepper. Heat 2 tablespoons oil in heavy large skillet over medium-high heat. Add fish and sear quickly on each side; do not crowd. Arrange fish over pasta. Sprinkle with snipped fresh chives and serve immediately.

Mussel Salad with Potatoes Vinaigrette

Light and fresh, with most of the preparation done ahead, this is the perfect change-of-pace dish. Precede with a lightly creamed carrot soup and follow with a hot apple tart. Pour a Soave, Muscadet or a fruity Beaujolais.

4 servings

2½ pounds mussels, scrubbed and debearded (discard any that are opened or broken)
1 tablespoon cornmeal
½ cup water
1½ pounds white rose, red or new potatoes

¼ cup cider vinegar
1 tablespoon olive oil
1 large shallot, minced
Salt and freshly ground pepper

¼ cup olive oil
4 to 5 large shallots, thinly sliced (about 1 cup)
1½ tablespoons chopped fresh basil or 1½ teaspoons dried, crumbled

1 teaspoon grated orange peel
2 large garlic cloves, minced (about 2 teaspoons)
1 teaspoon tomato paste

7 ounces fresh young spinach leaves, stemmed, rinsed and dried
4 large tomatoes, hollowed out and diced, or 8 canned plum tomatoes, seeded, drained and diced (2 cups diced)

3 tablespoons fresh lemon juice
Freshly ground pepper

Combine mussels in large bowl with enough cold water to cover. Sprinkle with cornmeal. Chill 8 to 24 hours.

Drain mussels. Transfer to 4-quart saucepan. Add ½ cup water, cover and place over medium-high heat. Cook until shells open, about 5 minutes. Remove opened mussels from pan using slotted spoon. Cook remaining mussels until opened, about 5 more minutes; discard any that do not open. Set mussels aside to cool; reserve liquid. Remove mussels from shells. Reserve about 6 shells for garnish; discard remaining shells. Refrigerate mussels in cooking liquid until ready to use. (*Can be prepared up to 24 hours ahead.*)

Combine potatoes in saucepan with enough water to cover. Place over medium-high heat and bring to boil. Let boil until potatoes are tender; cool *slightly*. Peel potatoes and slice into ⅛- to ¼-inch rounds; keep warm.

Place vinegar in large bowl. Whisk in 1 tablespoon olive oil 1 drop at a time. Add minced shallot with salt and pepper to taste. Add potatoes and toss gently to blend. Refrigerate until 2 hours before serving. (*Potatoes can be prepared up to 24 hours ahead.*)

About 30 minutes before serving, heat ¼ cup olive oil in heavy large non-aluminum skillet over medium-high heat. Add sliced shallot and sauté until soft, about 3 minutes. Stir in basil, orange peel and garlic and cook about 2 minutes, watching carefully so garlic does not brown. Blend in tomato paste and reserved mussel liquid and boil until reduced by ⅓. Set sauce aside.

Arrange spinach leaves in overlapping pattern on 12-inch round platter. Spoon potato salad into center. Bring sauce to boil over medium-high heat. Add diced tomato and cook 10 seconds. Reduce heat to medium, add reserved mussels and cook just until heated through; do not overcook or mussels will toughen. Stir in lemon juice. Season generously with pepper. Pour sauce over potatoes. Garnish with mussel shells. Serve at room temperature.

Charcuterie Salad

A good do-ahead recipe. This buffet or supper dish can be doubled easily. Crusty bread and beer or a light, dry wine are good companions.

4 to 6 servings

1 pound cooked well-marbled pork, trimmed of all fat and cut into thin sticks
¼ cup light olive oil
¼ cup Spanish Sherry vinegar
6 cornichons, cut into julienne
2 green onions, minced
1 large shallot, minced

1 pound new potatoes

¼ cup wine vinegar
3 tablespoons light olive oil

3 tablespoons minced sweet red onion
1 heaping teaspoon Dijon mustard
Salt and freshly ground pepper

1 large head romaine lettuce
1 cup julienne of roasted red bell peppers
2 green onions, cut into very thin 2-inch strips
1 tablespoon capers, rinsed and drained

Combine pork, ¼ cup oil, Sherry vinegar, cornichons, minced green onion and shallot in medium bowl and toss gently. Cover and refrigerate 1 to 2 days.

Boil potatoes in large saucepan in water to cover until tender. Drain well. Return to hot pan and place over heat to dry, shaking pan constantly. Let stand until cool enough to handle, then peel and cut into medium cubes.

Combine potatoes, wine vinegar, 3 tablespoons oil, red onion, mustard, salt and pepper in another bowl and toss lightly. Cover and refrigerate overnight.

To serve, arrange lettuce leaves on large platter, leaving center almost empty. Add peppers to pork mixture and toss well. Taste and season with salt and pepper. Arrange potato salad over lettuce in shallow ring and sprinkle with green onion. Mound pork in center; top with capers. Serve lightly chilled.

Warm Bernese Onion Salad

Don't look for lettuce in this robust country entrée. It is a one-dish meal of roasted potatoes, poached eggs, bratwurst and savory onions.

4 servings

2 teaspoons distilled white vinegar or cider vinegar
1 teaspoon salt
4 eggs, room temperature

2 tablespoons olive or vegetable oil
1 8-ounce slab smoked bacon, cut into ³/₈-inch cubes

4 large baking potatoes, unpeeled, cut into ¹/₂-inch rounds, soaked in cold water until ready to use
Freshly ground pepper

1¹/₄ pounds red onions, cut into ¹/₄-inch rings
1 tablespoon all purpose flour
1 teaspoon salt
¹/₂ teaspoon sugar
2 to 3 tablespoons white wine vinegar or cider vinegar
2 tablespoons rich beef stock

¹/₂ cup water
4 Swiss or German white bratwurst
2 tablespoons olive or vegetable oil

Fill heavy large skillet ²/₃ full with water. Add 2 teaspoons distilled vinegar and 1 teaspoon salt and bring to boil. Break eggs into skillet. Reduce heat to simmer and poach eggs until whites are firm (yolks should be soft), 3 to 4 minutes. Remove eggs with slotted spoon and place in bowl of cold water. When eggs are cool, trim edges with knife or scissors. Return to cold water.

Heat 2 tablespoons oil in heavy large skillet over medium heat. Add bacon and cook until drippings are rendered and bacon just begins to color, about 10 minutes; do not allow to crisp. Remove with slotted spoon and drain on paper towels. Cover bacon with foil. Pour drippings from skillet into small bowl and reserve. Return 4 tablespoons to skillet and set aside.

Position rack in center of oven and preheat to 375°F. Drain potato slices. Pat completely dry. Line baking sheet with foil. Brush with some of reserved bacon drippings. Arrange potato slices in single layer on prepared foil. Brush with drippings. Season with salt and pepper. Roast potatoes until puffed and golden brown, 30 to 35 minutes.

Meanwhile, heat remaining drippings in skillet over medium heat. Add onions and cook until translucent and just golden, stirring occasionally, about 5 minutes. Remove from heat. Sprinkle onions with flour, salt, sugar and pepper to taste. Return to heat and stir 3 minutes. Reduce heat to low. Add 2 tablespoons vinegar and stock and cook until syrupy, about 3 minutes. Adjust seasoning with additional 1 tablespoon vinegar if desired. Stir in bacon. Cover onions with foil and set aside until ready to serve.

Bring ¹/₂ cup water to boil in heavy medium skillet. Reduce heat, add bratwurst and simmer 5 minutes. Drain well. Heat 2 tablespoons oil in skillet. Add bratwurst and fry on all sides until crisp and golden brown.

Using slotted spoon, transfer poached eggs to bowl of warm water. Let stand until heated through, 2 minutes.

To serve, arrange roasted potato slices on warm plate. Top with poached egg. Surround with bratwurst and onions.

Salad of Ham, Gruyère and Cabbage in Roquefort Dressing

8 to 10 servings

½ cup red wine vinegar
1 tablespoon coarse-grained French mustard
1 large garlic clove, minced
1½ cups olive oil
⅓ cup crumbled Roquefort cheese, room temperature

1½ pounds cabbage, shredded
12 ounces baked ham, cut into ¾ × ¼-inch julienne

12 ounces Gruyère cheese, cut into ¾ × ¼-inch julienne, room temperature
6 tablespoons minced fresh parsley
Salt and freshly ground pepper
Bibb lettuce
1 to 2 truffles, grated (optional)

Blend vinegar, mustard and garlic in large bowl. Whisk in olive oil in thin stream. Stir in Roquefort until smooth. (*Can be prepared 1 day ahead and refrigerated. Stir before using.*)

Mix cabbage, ham, Gruyère and 4 tablespoons parsley into dressing. Season with salt and pepper. Arrange lettuce on platter. Mound salad in center. Sprinkle with remaining 2 tablespoons parsley and truffles if desired and serve immediately.

Victor Scocozza

Spinach and Raisin Pie

Seafood à la Mediterranée

Summer Seafood Blanquette
with Chard and Snow Peas

*Sauerkraut and Pork Gulyás
with Sour Cream*

Mongolian Hot Pot, Shanghai Style

Ratatouille with Sausage

5 ❦ Eggs and Cheese

Satisfying, versatile and thrifty, entrées based on eggs or cheese are also among the easiest to prepare of one-dish meals. Of course, eggs are particularly suited to brunch buffets; when the main dish boasts the multiple flavors and colors of Custom Omelet (page 61), Peloponnesus Tomato Omelet (page 60), or Huevos a la Flamenca (page 59), just add a pot of steaming coffee and a basket of rolls or croissants and the meal is complete.

Filled omelets are wonderfully adaptable. The Chicken-Vegetable Omelet on page 61, for example, is made with broccoli florets—but use a different vegetable, and meat or seafood instead of chicken, and *voilà*, a new dish. Farmer's Omelet (page 62), flavored with ham and dillweed, is a Swedish specialty—but substitute prosciutto and basil, or perhaps pepperoni and oregano, and the result brings Mediterranean sunshine to the table. Equally versatile is Mexicali One-Dish (page 58), an easy cheese casserole that can be varied at will by the addition of cooked meat, fish or poultry.

Their flexibility makes these dishes great additions to any cook's repertoire: With a few staple ingredients embellished by whatever fresh or cooked items you happen to have on hand, you can whip up a simple one-dish meal in no time.

Green Chili Cheese Pie

8 to 10 servings

¾ cup canned diced green chilies
12 ounces cheddar cheese, grated
12 ounces Monterey Jack
   cheese, grated
¼ teaspoon salt

Pinch of garlic powder
Dash of Worcestershire sauce
¼ cup diced onion
12 eggs, beaten

Preheat oven to 300°F. Lightly butter 9 × 13-inch baking dish. Spread ½ cup green chilies evenly over bottom of dish. Add cheeses and press firmly to form crust. Sprinkle with salt, garlic powder and Worcestershire sauce. Top with onion and remaining chilies. Spread eggs evenly over. Bake until partially set, about 25 to 30 minutes. Turn off oven, open door and let pie cool 10 minutes to set. Cut evenly into squares and serve warm or at room temperature.

Mexicali One-Dish

Serve this with a tossed green salad for a light meatless supper.

4 to 6 servings

3 cups sour cream
2 4-ounce cans diced green chilies
   Worcestershire sauce
   Salt

4 cups cooked long-grain rice
1 pound Monterey Jack
   cheese, diced
½ to ¾ cup grated cheddar cheese

Preheat oven to 300°F. Butter 3-quart baking dish. Combine sour cream, chilies, Worcestershire and salt in large bowl. Spread ⅓ of rice in bottom of dish. Spread half of sour cream mixture evenly over top and sprinkle with half of Jack cheese. Repeat layering, ending with remaining rice. Sprinkle top with cheddar cheese. Bake until cheese is melted and casserole is heated through, about 45 minutes. Serve immediately.
   For variation, add cooked chicken, beef, pork, turkey, lamb or tuna.

Marion's Chili Relleno Burritos

12 servings

5 tablespoons butter
1 medium onion, finely chopped
2 cups (1 pint) sour cream
¼ teaspoon cayenne pepper
   Pinch of salt
   Pinch of freshly ground pepper
1 15-ounce can refried beans

4 eggs, beaten to blend
12 canned whole green chilies
3 cups grated Monterey Jack cheese

12 8-inch flour tortillas
12 avocado slices
   Mild or hot salsa

Melt 2 tablespoons butter in medium skillet over medium heat. Add onion and sauté until soft, 5 to 7 minutes. Stir in 2 tablespoons sour cream, cayenne, salt and pepper. Mix in refried beans. Remove from heat, cover and keep warm.
   Melt 1 tablespoon butter in another medium skillet over medium heat. Pour ⅓ of eggs into skillet. Arrange 4 chilies over eggs in half of pan. Sprinkle with 1 cup cheese. Cook until just set, about 2 minutes. Fold other half over (as for omelet) and cook until firmly set, about 1 minute. Slice into 4 pieces, cutting between chilies. Keep warm. Repeat twice.
   Warm tortillas in dry skillet over medium heat, 1 minute per side. Fill each with egg strip, bean mixture, sour cream and avocado slice. Add salsa to taste. Roll up, then fold in edges. Serve burritos immediately.

Sharp Bread Pudding

Serve this easy-to-prepare entrée with a salad for Sunday supper.

6 servings

4 extra-large eggs
1/3 cup milk
8 slices firm-textured white bread
12 ounces mozzarella cheese, thinly sliced

4 ounces Emmenthal cheese, thinly sliced
4 to 8 ounces thinly sliced ham
Freshly ground pepper

Preheat oven to 350°F. Generously butter 8-inch square baking dish. Beat eggs with milk in shallow dish to combine. Soak 4 bread slices in egg mixture 2 minutes. Arrange soaked bread in prepared baking dish in single layer. Add remaining bread to egg mixture. Cover bread in baking dish with half of mozzarella and half of Emmenthal. Cover cheese with ham. Layer on remaining cheese and sprinkle with pepper. Top cheese with remaining bread in single layer, pouring on any remaining egg mixture. Bake bread pudding until top is light brown and cheese bubbles, about 40 minutes. Serve hot.

Egg, Sausage and Apple Brunch

4 to 6 servings

1 pound pork sausage meat
6 large pippin apples, peeled, cored and thickly sliced
2 tablespoons sugar
1/4 teaspoon cinnamon

2 tablespoons (1/4 stick) butter
6 eggs, beaten to blend

Shape sausage into 3-inch patties. Cook in large dry skillet over medium-high heat until browned, about 7 minutes per side. Pour off fat in skillet. Reduce heat to medium. Add apples, sprinkle with sugar and cinnamon and cook until softened, stirring frequently, about 10 minutes. Transfer mixture to serving platter and keep warm.

Melt butter in medium skillet over low heat. Add eggs and scramble to desired firmness. Add to platter and serve.

Huevos a la Flamenca (Eggs Andalusian Style)

This recipe comes from Seville's elegant Hotel Alfonso XIII—a bit ironic, perhaps, considering the earthiness of the dish. It is a very colorful entrée and a perfect choice for either a brunch or lunch buffet. Except for the finishing touches, it can be prepared well ahead of time and needs only a fast 15 minutes in the oven.

6 servings

5 tablespoons olive oil
2 medium-size yellow onions, chopped
2 large garlic cloves, minced
1 teaspoon dried basil, crumbled
1/2 teaspoon dried marjoram, crumbled
1/2 teaspoon dried thyme, crumbled
1 28-ounce can Italian-style tomatoes packed in puree
1 8-ounce can tomato sauce
1/4 cup dry white wine

2 medium-size red or green bell peppers, sliced into 6 rings total, seeded and cored (trimmings reserved)

6 medium boiling potatoes, boiled until tender, cooled, peeled and cut into 1/2-inch cubes

4 ounces prosciutto, diced
4 ounces pepperoni, thinly sliced, sautéed in 2 tablespoons unsalted butter 5 minutes and drained well

1/2 cup fresh or frozen green peas, cooked and drained
6 small eggs
10 parboiled or canned white asparagus tips

Heat 2 tablespoons olive oil in large skillet over medium heat. Add onions and garlic and cook, stirring constantly, until onions are limp, about 5 to 8 minutes. Add basil, marjoram and thyme and continue cooking 1 to 2 minutes. Add tomatoes with puree (breaking up large pieces), tomato sauce and wine. Reduce heat to low and simmer 1 hour, stirring occasionally.

Meanwhile, heat remaining 3 tablespoons olive oil in large skillet over medium heat. Add pepper rings and sauté until limp, about 5 minutes. Drain on paper towels. Mince pepper trimmings and sauté in same oil until limp, about 5 minutes. Add potatoes and toss thoroughly.

Preheat oven to 400°F (375°F for glass). Spoon potato mixture into bottom of shallow 2- to 2½-quart earthenware or glass baking dish. Top with prosciutto and pepperoni. Pour tomato mixture over top. (*Can be prepared 2 to 3 hours ahead to this point and refrigerated. Let stand at room temperature 45 minutes before baking.*)

Sprinkle peas over tomato mixture. Place 1 pepper ring in center and arrange remaining 5 rings around edge. Make 6 depressions in surface of tomato mixture with back of spoon. Carefully break eggs into each depression. Arrange asparagus tips in pairs spoke-fashion between pepper rings. Bake until bubbly and egg whites begin to set, about 10 to 15 minutes. Stir eggs into tomato mixture (this finishes cooking them) and serve immediately.

Peloponnesus Tomato Omelet

The eggs are cooked until set, so the finished dish resembles a frittata.

6 servings

¼ cup olive oil
5 green onions (including 3 inches of green tops), chopped
6 small or 3 large ripe tomatoes, peeled and sliced ⅓ inch thick
Salt and freshly ground pepper

1 cup grated mizithra, hard ricotta or dry Monterey Jack cheese (3 ounces)

1 tablespoon chopped fresh oregano or 1 teaspoon dried, crumbled
9 eggs, beaten to blend
¼ cup minced fresh parsley

Heat oil in heavy large broilerproof slope-sided skillet over medium heat. Add onions and cook until soft, about 10 minutes, stirring occasionally. Arrange layer of tomatoes over onions. Season with salt and pepper. Cover and simmer until tomatoes are tender, about 10 minutes, uncovering for last few minutes of cooking if necessary to evaporate excess liquid.

Sprinkle cheese and oregano over tomatoes. Reduce heat to low, pour eggs over and cook without stirring until eggs are almost set, about 9 minutes.

Position rack 6 inches from heat source and preheat broiler. Place skillet under broiler until eggs are completely set and top of omelet is golden brown, about 2 minutes. Slide omelet out onto serving platter. Top with parsley. Cut into wedges to serve.

Custom Omelet

6 to 8 servings

3 tablespoons butter
8 bacon slices, chopped
1 medium-size green bell pepper, seeded and diced
1 small onion, diced

4 ounces cooked ham or chicken, diced
½ cup cooked fresh artichoke hearts or canned, drained

¼ cup halved black olives
¼ cup halved green olives
8 eggs
½ can beer, room temperature
Pinch of paprika
Salt and freshly ground pepper
1½ cups grated mozzarella cheese
Sliced tomatoes

Melt butter in large cast-iron skillet over medium heat. Add bacon and fry until just cooked but not crisp, about 5 minutes. Add bell pepper and onion and sauté until onion is translucent, about 10 minutes. Remove from heat; cool slightly.

Preheat oven to 450°F. Spread bell pepper mixture evenly over bottom of skillet. Sprinkle ham, artichoke hearts and olives over bell pepper mixture. Beat eggs with beer, paprika, salt and pepper. Pour into skillet. Sprinkle with cheese. Bake until center is firm, about 25 minutes. Cut into wedges, garnish with tomato slices and serve.

Chicken-Vegetable Omelet

4 servings

Filling
2 tablespoons (¼ stick) butter
3 tablespoons all purpose flour
1 cup chicken stock
½ cup whipping cream
8 ounces broccoli florets, blanched until crisp-tender
8 ounces spinach, stemmed, shredded and blanched 1 minute
1 cup shredded cooked chicken

½ teaspoon freshly ground white pepper
Salt

Omelet
7 eggs
¼ cup water
½ teaspoon salt
Freshly ground white pepper
2 teaspoons butter

For filling: Melt butter in heavy medium saucepan over medium-low heat. Whisk in flour and cook 3 minutes. Gradually whisk in stock and cream and boil until thickened. Stir in broccoli, spinach, chicken and pepper. Season with salt to taste and keep warm.

For omelet: Whisk eggs, water, salt and pepper until well blended. Melt butter in 10-inch omelet pan or heavy skillet over medium-high heat. Add egg mixture. Using spatula, lift eggs as they cook, letting uncooked part run underneath until omelet is cooked but still creamy. Spoon ¾ of filling onto half of omelet. Slide out onto platter, folding empty half over filled half. Spoon remaining filling over. Cut into wedges. Serve immediately.

Farmer's Omelet

4 servings

¼ cup (½ stick) butter
4 medium boiling potatoes, peeled and cut into ¼-inch cubes
1 medium onion, thinly sliced
6 ounces ham, finely diced
2 tablespoons snipped fresh chives
½ teaspoon dried dillweed

6 eggs
½ cup milk

1 teaspoon salt
½ teaspoon freshly ground pepper

1 cup shredded Monterey Jack cheese
1 medium tomato, peeled and sliced
1 medium-size green bell pepper, thinly sliced into rings
1 cup sour cream

Melt butter in 10-inch omelet pan or heavy skillet over medium heat. Add potatoes and onion and cook until tender, stirring often, 20 to 25 minutes. Add ham, chives and dillweed.

Whisk eggs, milk, salt and pepper until well blended. Pour over potato mixture. Reduce heat to low, cover and cook until egg mixture is set, 15 to 20 minutes; do not overcook.

Preheat broiler. Sprinkle omelet with half of cheese. Arrange tomato and green pepper over. Sprinkle with remaining cheese. Broil until cheese melts. Serve omelet hot with sour cream.

Huevos Rancheros

4 servings

1 tablespoon butter
4 eggs
½ cup finely chopped tomato
¼ cup finely minced green onion
¼ cup finely minced green bell pepper

⅔ cup grated Monterey Jack cheese
2 to 3 tablespoons hot taco sauce
1 medium avocado, thinly sliced

Melt butter in 10-inch skillet over medium heat. Break eggs into skillet. Add tomato, onion and bell pepper. Sprinkle with cheese. Top with taco sauce. Cover and cook until whites are set, 5 to 7 minutes. Top with avocado and serve.

Shrimp Huevos Rancheros

In this variation on a favorite dish, puffy corn tortillas are stuffed with a savory shrimp and egg filling.

12 servings

5 to 6 tablespoons butter
24 small to medium shrimp, halved horizontally, or 1½ cups sliced lobster or langostino
8 green onions (with 1½ inches green), thinly sliced
4 fresh green chilies (Anaheim or poblano), roasted, peeled, seeded and cut into ½ × 1-inch strips

8 eggs, beaten to blend
1 teaspoon salt or to taste
6 tablespoons sour cream, room temperature
12 tortillas*
Sliced green onion (garnish)
Southwest Tomato Sauce (see following recipe)

Melt butter in medium skillet over medium-high heat. Add shrimp, onions and chilies and sauté just until shrimp turn pink, about 1½ minutes. Reduce heat to medium-low, add eggs and gently scramble until just set. Season with salt. Stir in sour cream. Remove from heat. Using sharp knife, cut slit in side of tortilla, forming pocket. Spoon in egg mixture, dividing evenly. Transfer to platter. Sprinkle with onion. Pass sauce separately.

*Tortillas

Makes 12 to 15

2 cups instant masa mix	1 teaspoon salt
¼ cup stone-ground cornmeal	1 cup warm water
1½ teaspoons sugar	(or more if necessary)
1 teaspoon solid vegetable shortening	Peanut oil (for deep frying)
1 teaspoon baking powder	

Combine masa mix, cornmeal, sugar, shortening, baking powder and salt in processor. With machine running, pour 1 cup warm water through feed tube in slow steady stream. Stop machine and test: Mixture should be texture of stiff cookie dough. If too stiff, continue mixing, adding 3 to 4 more tablespoons water one at a time until dough attains correct texture and forms loose ball. Pinch off walnut-size piece of dough and roll into ball (if dough is too dry, it will crack and will be difficult to shape; if too moist, it will stick). Return test piece of dough to processor and mix in small amounts of additional water or masa mix as necessary.

Remove dough from processor and pat into ball. Cover tightly with plastic wrap. Let rest at room temperature at least 30 minutes or up to several hours.

Pour oil into large saucepan or deep fryer to depth of 2½ inches and heat to 375°F. Lay piece of plastic wrap over saucer. Pinch off walnut-size piece of dough and roll into ball. Set ball in center of saucer. Top with another piece of plastic, then another saucer. Press down on saucer gently to flatten dough to 4½- to 5-inch circle. Peel plastic wrap away from dough (do not peel dough away from plastic or circle will crumble). Immerse dough in hot oil; immediately begin spooning oil over top and cook until puffed and brown, about 1 minute. Remove from pan using slotted spoon and drain on paper towels (if dough appears un-cooked, ball is too large). Repeat with remaining dough.

Tortillas can be prepared up to 1 hour ahead and set aside.

Southwest Tomato Sauce

This sauce can be made well ahead of time and re-heated before serving.

Makes 1 quart

4 to 5 large fresh tomatoes or one 28-ounce can Italian plum tomatoes, broken up with fork	6 tablespoons tomato paste
	6 medium basil leaves or 4 to 5 cilantro sprigs
¼ cup vegetable or olive oil	1 teaspoon salt
1 medium onion, finely minced	Freshly ground pepper
½ green bell pepper, finely minced	¾ cup loosely packed fresh parsley or cilantro, finely minced
2 garlic cloves, minced	
½ cup red wine vinegar	

Cut out stem end of tomatoes (do not core). Broil tomatoes 4 inches from heat source until skin is softened, turning occasionally. Place in processor or blender and puree until smooth.

Heat oil in medium skillet over medium-high heat. Add onion, bell pepper and garlic and sauté until beginning to soften, 3 to 4 minutes. Add tomatoes and blend well. Stir in vinegar, tomato paste, basil, salt and pepper. Simmer until sauce is medium-thick, 8 to 10 minutes. Stir in parsley or cilantro. Serve sauce warm or at room temperature.

Poached Eggs in Spicy Salsa with Cheese on Fried Corn Tortillas

A bit of chocolate balances the acidity of the tomatoes. Even more chili can be added for a spicier version.

6 servings

Green Salsa

2¼ pounds green tomatoes, cut into 8 pieces each
2 green bell peppers, cut into 8 pieces each
1 large onion, chopped
5 fresh parsley sprigs, tied together
3 jalapeño peppers, seeded and chopped
2 garlic cloves, chopped
1 teaspoon ground coriander
1 teaspoon ground cumin
1 teaspoon salt
¼ teaspoon dried oregano, crumbled
Freshly ground pepper
1 tablespoon butter
2 teaspoons finely chopped bittersweet or semisweet chocolate

½ cup vegetable oil
12 fresh corn tortillas (see page 63)
Salt

6 extra-large eggs
2 cups grated Monterey Jack cheese (about 6 ounces)

For salsa: Combine first 11 ingredients in heavy medium saucepan over low heat. Cover and cook until vegetables are very soft, stirring occasionally, about 30 minutes. Uncover, increase heat and simmer until sauce mounds in spoon, stirring frequently, about 1 hour. Discard parsley. Puree sauce through food mill, discarding seeds and peels. Whisk butter and chocolate into sauce. (*Can be prepared 1 day ahead. Cover tightly and refrigerate.*)

Heat oil in large skillet to 375°F. Add tortillas in batches (do not crowd) and cook until golden brown and crisp, about 30 seconds on each side. Drain on paper towels. Sprinkle with salt.

Meanwhile, bring salsa to simmer in heavy large skillet. Break eggs into salsa. Cover each with cheese. Cover and poach eggs until set, about 3 minutes.

Arrange 1 tortilla on each plate. Spoon 1 egg with surrounding sauce and melted cheese atop each. Serve immediately, passing remaining tortillas.

6 ❧ Seafood

For too long many American diners have shied away from cooking fish and shellfish at home, opting instead to dine at nautically decorated oyster bars and lobster shacks. Fortunately this is changing as we learn how easy seafood is to prepare—and how perfect it is for those of us who are trying to keep weight and cholesterol counts under some kind of control.

But cooks from other parts of the world have been preparing luscious fish and shellfish specialties for generations, and this assortment of one-dish entrées reflects seafood's global appeal. Northern Europe is represented in such dishes as Braised Seafood Armorica (page 73), Jansson's Temptation (page 67), and potato-topped English Fish Pie (page 71), while in the Mediterranean style you will find Lemon Fish with Vegetables and Parsley Sauce (page 66), Seafood à la Mediterranée (page 70), and Shrimp and Sweet Peppers (page 76). Oriental flavors appear too, in Seafood Wok (page 69) and Ginger Shrimp with Pea Pods (page 76).

Most of these succulent mixtures are best complemented by nothing more than steamed rice or a crusty loaf of bread to soak up their tasty sauces. And because fish and shellfish take only minutes to cook, there are plenty of ideas here for colorful and delicious one-dish dinners to prepare even when time is short.

Lemon Fish with Vegetables and Parsley Sauce

A superb entrée in the Greek style.

12 servings

¾ cup fresh lemon juice
2 generous teaspoons dried oregano, crumbled
Salt and freshly ground pepper
1 8-pound or two 4-pound whole fish (such as cod, sea bass, sea trout or pike)

2 cups dry white wine
½ cup olive oil
1 garlic clove, minced
10 medium-size new potatoes, peeled and cut into 1½-inch slices

8 to 12 medium carrots, peeled and cut into 1-inch slices
1½ pounds pearl onions, peeled
1 celery stalk, cut into 1-inch slices

1 tablespoon cornstarch mixed with ½ cup water
20 green Greek olives
Lemon wedges and fresh dill sprigs
Parsley Sauce*

Blend lemon juice, oregano, salt and pepper in container large enough for fish. Add fish and marinate at room temperature 2 hours, turning occasionally.

Bring 1 cup wine, oil and garlic to boil in fish poacher over medium-high heat. Add potatoes, carrots, onions and celery. Cover and cook until vegetables are tender; check frequently and add water to poacher as necessary. Remove each vegetable as it is done.

Arrange fish on piece of cheesecloth that is several times width of fish. Pour marinade into poacher. Blend in remaining wine with enough water to cover fish. Holding sides of cheesecloth, lower fish into poacher. Place over medium-high heat and bring to boil. Reduce heat so liquid is just shaking, cover partially and poach until fish is tender, turning once, about 9 minutes total per inch of thickness.

Transfer fish to platter. Increase heat and reduce poaching liquid to 1½ cups. Whisk in cornstarch mixture and cook until thickened to desired consistency; do not boil. Strain liquid. Pour over fish. Arrange vegetables around fish. Garnish with olives, lemon and dill. Serve chilled or at room temperature with sauce.

*Parsley Sauce

This sauce can double as a dip. Simply add slightly more oil to the running processor and mix until thickened.

Makes 3 generous cups

12 ⅜-inch-thick slices white bread, crusts trimmed
2 bunches parsley, stemmed
¼ cup fresh lemon juice
1 very small onion
2 tablespoons vinegar
Salt

3 cups corn oil
4 egg yolks, room temperature
¼ cup milk
Freshly ground pepper

Soak bread in water, then squeeze dry. Transfer to processor. Add parsley, lemon juice, onion and vinegar with salt to taste and mix until creamy. With machine running, add oil through feed tube in slow steady stream until sauce is consistency of thin mayonnaise. Mix in yolks. Blend in milk. Add pepper to taste. Refrigerate 4 to 5 hours. Serve chilled. Sauce will thicken on standing.

Jansson's Temptation (Jansson's Frestelse)

A Finnish dish served as either main course or side dish.

8 servings

6 large baking potatoes, peeled and cut as for French fries
3 medium onions, thinly sliced
8 ounces pickled herring fillets, drained

1½ cups whipping cream
1 egg, beaten to blend
1½ teaspoons salt
1 teaspoon freshly ground pepper

Preheat oven to 250°F. Butter one 4-quart or two 2-quart casseroles or baking dishes. Layer potatoes, onions and herring in casserole(s). Blend cream, egg, salt and pepper. Pour over herring. Cover with foil. Bake until almost all liquid is absorbed and potatoes and onions are just tender, about 2¼ hours. Uncover and continue baking until all liquid is absorbed and top is lightly browned, about 45 more minutes. Serve immediately.

Salmon-Corn Casserole

4 servings

2 17-ounce cans cream-style corn
1 15-ounce can red or pink salmon, drained and flaked
3 eggs
⅓ cup cracker crumbs (reserve 1 tablespoon for topping)

1 teaspoon salt
¼ teaspoon freshly ground pepper
Butter

Preheat oven to 350°F. Butter 1½-quart baking dish. Combine all ingredients except butter and reserved crumbs in large bowl and mix well. Turn into prepared dish. Sprinkle with remaining cracker crumbs. Dot with butter. Bake until set, about 1 hour. Serve immediately.

Colombo de Poisson (Curried Fish Stew)

This dish hails from Martinique in the French West Indies. Colombo, a mixture of spices, reflects Indian influences on the local cuisine.

4 servings

1 quart water
1 cup dry white wine
6 whole black peppercorns
1½ pounds fresh shark, tuna or other firm fish, cut into 1-inch cubes

¼ cup peanut oil
2 medium onions, chopped
Colombo*
1 teaspoon all purpose flour

1½ cups chicken stock
½ cup coconut cream
2 tablespoons fresh lime juice
2 tablespoons dark rum
Salt and freshly ground pepper
Freshly cooked rice
Sliced green onion

Bring water, wine and peppercorns to simmer in heavy medium saucepan. Add fish and adjust heat until liquid barely shimmers. Cook fish until just opaque. Transfer to bowl using slotted spoon; discard liquid.

Heat oil in heavy large skillet over medium heat. Add onions and cook until translucent, stirring frequently, about 8 minutes. Add colombo and flour and stir 3 minutes. Whisk in stock. Cook until sauce thickens slightly, stirring occasionally, about 5 minutes. Puree sauce in blender or processor until smooth. Return to skillet. Mix in coconut cream, lime juice, rum, salt and pepper and warm over medium heat. Stir in fish and reheat. Spoon over rice in shallow bowls. Sprinkle with green onion. Serve immediately.

*Colombo

Makes about 2 tablespoons

1 small whole dried red chili
1 teaspoon ground coriander
1 teaspoon dry mustard

⅛ teaspoon turmeric
3 garlic cloves, mashed

Pulverize chili, coriander, mustard and turmeric in mortar with pestle. Work in garlic until paste forms.

Santa Fe Seafood Stew

4 to 6 servings

6 large dried New Mexico chilies, seeded
2 large dried ancho chilies, seeded
6 cups fish stock or clam juice

2 tablespoons olive oil
1 large onion, diced
1 pound monkfish or bass, cut into 1-inch chunks
20 small clams, scrubbed
1 large garlic clove, minced

2 2½-pound crabs (top shells removed), cleaned and quartered
1 pound cooked small unpeeled red potatoes, diced
1 pound unshelled jumbo shrimp
1 tablespoon fresh lime juice
Salt and freshly ground pepper
Cilantro leaves
Lime slices

Soak chilies in fish stock until softened, about 30 minutes. Transfer mixture to blender and puree.

Heat oil in heavy large saucepan over medium-low heat. Add onion and cook until transparent, stirring occasionally, about 10 minutes. Add pureed chilies, monkfish, clams and garlic and bring to boil. Reduce heat, cover and cook until clams open, about 3 minutes. Add crab, potatoes and shrimp and cook until shrimp turn pink. Add lime juice. Adjust seasoning with salt and pepper. Ladle into bowls. Garnish with cilantro and lime slices. Serve immediately.

Luxurious Crab and Artichoke Casserole

10 to 12 servings

½ cup (1 stick) butter
3 tablespoons minced onion
½ cup all purpose flour
4 cups (1 quart) whipping cream, heated to boiling
½ cup Madeira
Salt and freshly ground pepper

2 tablespoons fresh lemon juice
4 cups fresh or canned crabmeat

3 9-ounce packages frozen artichoke hearts, cooked according to package directions
2½ cups shell macaroni, cooked and drained
2 cups grated Gruyère or Swiss cheese
Paprika (optional)

Preheat oven to 350°F. Melt butter in heavy large skillet. When butter sizzles, add onion and sauté until golden. Stir in flour and cook over low heat until flour is pale yellow. Remove from heat. Add cream, stirring vigorously. Return to medium heat and stir until sauce comes to boil. Reduce heat and add Madeira. Season with salt and pepper. Remove from heat.

Butter 6-quart casserole. Pour lemon juice over crabmeat; toss lightly. Combine crab, artichoke hearts, macaroni and sauce in casserole. Sprinkle with cheese and dust with paprika, if desired. Bake for 25 to 30 minutes, or until heated through. Serve immediately.

Casserole can be prepared a day ahead and refrigerated. Bring to room temperature before placing in preheated oven.

Seafood Feta Casserole

Serve this flavorful dish over orzo (rice-shaped pasta) for a hearty meal.

6 servings

2 tablespoons olive oil
1 pound pearl onions, peeled
2 large garlic cloves, minced
1 28-ounce can stewed tomatoes (undrained)
1/2 cup dry white wine
3 tablespoons chopped fresh parsley
3/4 teaspoon dried oregano, crumbled
Freshly ground pepper

1 pound fresh cod, scrod, haddock or halibut, cut into 3/4-inch pieces
4 ounces medium shrimp, peeled and deveined, room temperature
8 ounces feta cheese, cut into chunks

Heat oil in 3-quart saucepan over medium-high heat. Add onions and sauté until browned, about 5 minutes. Add garlic and sauté 10 seconds. Increase heat to high and stir in tomatoes with liquid, wine, 2 tablespoons parsley, oregano and pepper. Bring to boil. Reduce heat, cover and simmer 10 minutes, stirring occasionally. (*Can be prepared 1 day ahead and refrigerated. Bring to room temperature before using.*)

Preheat oven to 400°F. Pour tomato mixture into 2½-quart casserole. Top with fish. Cover and bake 10 minutes. Add shrimp to casserole. Sprinkle with feta cheese. Continue baking until fish is opaque and shrimp are cooked through, about 10 minutes. Sprinkle with remaining 1 tablespoon parsley and serve.

Seafood Wok

6 servings

1/2 cup peanut oil
1½ pounds sea scallops
12 jumbo shrimp, shelled and deveined
4 garlic cloves, minced
2 teaspoons minced fresh ginger
2 tablespoons dry Sherry
6 cups mixed fresh vegetables (broccoli, cauliflower, cabbage, Napa cabbage and carrot), cut into 1/4-inch slices

1½ pounds firm-fleshed white fish fillets, cut into 1/2-inch-wide slices
1½ cups hot fish stock or water
2 tablespoons soy sauce
2 tablespoons cornstarch
1 tablespoon sugar
2 teaspoons oriental sesame oil
2 dashes hot pepper sauce
Freshly cooked rice

Heat wok over high heat for 30 seconds. Add peanut oil, swirl to coat sides of wok and heat 15 more seconds. Add scallops and shrimp and stir-fry 2 minutes. Add garlic and ginger and stir-fry 10 seconds. Stir in Sherry. Add vegetables and fish fillets and stir-fry 30 seconds. Blend in stock. Cover tightly and cook 2 minutes. Meanwhile, combine soy sauce and cornstarch in cup. Stir into wok with sugar, sesame oil and pepper sauce and cook, stirring, until thickened. Serve immediately with rice.

Seafood à la Mediterranée

4 to 6 servings

½ cup olive oil
4 medium garlic cloves, minced
12 cherrystone or littleneck clams, scrubbed
3 lobster tails (about 1½-pounds total), cut into 1-inch segments (shells intact) and patted dry
12 jumbo shrimp, deveined (shells intact) and patted dry
1 cup dry white wine (preferably Chablis), warmed

2 cups drained canned Italian plum tomatoes
2 bay leaves
½ teaspoon dried oregano, crumbled
Salt and freshly ground pepper
3 cups steamed white rice
2 tablespoons chopped fresh parsley

Heat oil in deep heavy skillet over medium-high heat. Add garlic and sauté 1 minute; do not brown. Add clams and lobster and sauté 1 minute. Add shrimp and sauté 1 minute. Pour in wine and simmer until lobster and shrimp are just opaque, 2 to 3 minutes. Remove lobster and shrimp from broth using slotted spoon; set aside. Add tomatoes, bay leaves and oregano with salt and pepper to taste. Simmer until clams open, 2 to 3 minutes; discard any that do not open. Discard bay leaves. Return lobster and shrimp to stew. Spoon bed of rice into heated rimmed bowls. Ladle stew over rice. Sprinkle with parsley and serve.

California Cioppino

Cioppino, a Bay Area favorite, is really nothing more than bouillabaisse gone West. It has its origins in the hearty seafood stews of the Mediterranean, the region responsible for many of the culinary traditions that were transplanted to California by the Italian-Americans who pioneered the northern part of the state.

2 servings

¼ cup olive oil
¼ cup chopped green bell pepper
¼ cup chopped fresh parsley
1 small onion, chopped
1 celery stalk, chopped
1 garlic clove, minced
1 28-ounce can Italian plum tomatoes (undrained)
½ cup dry white wine
½ cup tomato sauce
1 tablespoon dried porcini mushrooms (optional), softened in hot water, drained and chopped

½ teaspoon dried basil, crumbled
1 bay leaf
Pinch of cayenne pepper
Salt and freshly ground pepper

8 ounces firm-fleshed white fish, cut into large chunks
4 ounces shrimp or prawns, shelled except for tails, deveined

1 2-pound cooked Dungeness crab

Heat oil in Dutch oven or casserole over medium-low heat. Add bell pepper, parsley, onion, celery and garlic and cook until onion is translucent, stirring occasionally, about 10 minutes. Add tomatoes with liquid, wine, tomato sauce, mushrooms, basil, bay leaf, cayenne and salt and pepper and bring to boil. Reduce heat, cover and simmer gently 2 hours.

Add fish and shrimp to sauce. Simmer 20 minutes; do not stir.

Meanwhile, crack crab legs; do not shell. Remove meat from body and cut into large chunks. Add crab legs and meat to sauce and cook until heated through. Serve immediately.

English Fish Pie

6 to 8 servings

2 pounds scrod fillets
8 ounces bay scallops
5 parsley sprigs
1 lemon, quartered
  Water
  Dry white wine

4 pounds baking potatoes, peeled
  and quartered
6 tablespoons (¾ stick) butter
8 tablespoons milk
  Salt and freshly ground pepper

6 tablespoons (¾ stick) butter
½ cup all purpose flour
1 cup milk
  Salt and freshly ground pepper
  Dry white wine (optional)
  Fresh lemon juice (optional)
  Minced fresh parsley (optional)

Place scrod, scallops, parsley sprigs and lemon in heavy large skillet. Cover ⅔ way up ingredients with water and remaining ⅓ with wine. Cover skillet with tight-filling lid or buttered waxed paper. Set over high heat and bring to boil. Reduce heat and simmer until fish is barely cooked, about 3 minutes. Drain, reserving cooking liquid. Discard parsley and lemon. Remove as many bones as possible from scrod. Let seafood mixture cool completely.

Cook potatoes in large amount of boiling salted water until tender. Drain. Mash through sieve into bowl with mallet, using straight up and down motion to prevent stickiness. Beat in 6 tablespoons butter and 2 tablespoons milk using electric mixer. Add 6 tablespoons milk and continue beating until mixture is quite stiff. Season with salt and freshly ground pepper.

Melt remaining 6 tablespoons butter in heavy medium saucepan over medium-low heat. Sprinkle with flour and whisk 3 minutes. Gradually add remaining 1 cup milk, whisking until mixture comes to boil and thickens. Whisk in enough fish cooking liquid to thin sauce to consistency of whipping cream. Season to taste with salt and pepper. Add wine, lemon juice and parsley if desired.

Preheat oven to 325°F. Arrange scrod and scallops in 8 × 12-inch glass or ceramic baking dish. Pour sauce over. Let cool 10 minutes. Spoon mashed potatoes into pastry bag fitted with ¾-inch sawtooth tip and pipe over seafood. Bake pie for 30 minutes.

Preheat broiler. Place pie under broiler until top is brown. Serve immediately.

Summer Seafood Blanquette with Chard and Snow Peas

*For this colorful stew,
sea bass can be substituted
for salmon.*

4 servings

2 cups fish stock
½ cup dry white wine
8 jumbo shrimp, shelled and
  deveined, shells reserved
1 cup whipping cream
  Salt and freshly ground pepper
12 ounces salmon fillet (small bones
  removed), skinned and cut into
  1-inch cubes
4 ounces small sea scallops,
  trimmed

8 ounces Swiss chard, stemmed,
  halved lengthwise, cut crosswise
  into ½-inch strips and blanched
  3 minutes
8 ounces snow peas, trimmed and
  blanched 1 minute
1 tablespoon minced fresh tarragon
1 tablespoon snipped fresh chives
1 tablespoon minced fresh parsley

Bring stock, wine and shells to boil in heavy medium saucepan. Reduce heat and simmer gently 15 minutes. Strain liquid into heavy large skillet; discard shells. Add half of cream and bring to simmer, stirring. Season with salt and pepper.

Reduce heat to low. Add shrimp and cook 1 minute. Turn shrimp over. Add salmon and scallops and cook until just tender, about 4 minutes, shaking pan occasionally. Remove seafood using slotted spoon. Divide among shallow bowls.

Boil sauce until reduced to 1 cup. Whisk in remaining cream and boil until sauce is thick enough to coat back of spoon, about 10 minutes. Stir in chard and peas and heat through. Remove from heat. Stir in herbs. Adjust seasoning. Pour off any liquid exuded from seafood. Transfer vegetables to bowls using slotted spoon. Pour sauce over. Serve immediately.

Le Pot-au-Feu de Poisson à l'Ail Doux

This elegant version of pot-au-feu is from the Four Seasons Olympic Hotel in Seattle.

4 servings

Delicate Garlic Sauce
3 large garlic cloves
¾ cup fish stock
¾ cup dry white wine
3 shallots, minced
2 cups whipping cream
Salt

12 asparagus tips

2 cups fish stock
2 cups water
4 new potatoes, halved
4 small leeks, cut into 2-inch pieces
4 small onions, halved
3 small turnips, peeled and cut into quarters
8 baby carrots, peeled

2 cups fish stock
1 cup dry white wine
8 crayfish
8 mussels, scrubbed and debearded
8 large prawns, shelled and deveined
1 8-ounce salmon fillet, cut into 4 pieces
1 8-ounce John Dory or sea bass fillet, cut into 4 pieces
8 ounces sea scallops

1 tablespoon snipped fresh chives

For sauce: Cover garlic with cold water in small saucepan. Bring to boil. Drain. Repeat 5 times. Press garlic through strainer to puree. Boil stock, wine and shallots in heavy medium saucepan until reduced to 2 tablespoons, about 20 minutes. Add cream and simmer until reduced to 1½ cups, about 15 minutes. Mix in pureed garlic. Season with salt. (*Can be prepared 4 hours ahead and refrigerated.*)

Blanch asparagus in boiling salted water until just crisp-tender. Rinse under cold water and drain.

Bring 2 cups stock and 2 cups water to boil in large saucepan. Add potatoes, leeks, onions, turnips and carrots. Bring to boil. Reduce heat and simmer until vegetables are tender, about 15 minutes. Drain, reserving cooking liquid. (*Can be prepared 4 hours ahead.*)

Just before serving, reheat vegetables and asparagus in reserved cooking liquid. Transfer to warm platter using slotted spoon and tent with foil.

Meanwhile, bring 2 cups stock and 1 cup wine to boil in large skillet. Add crayfish. Cover and simmer 2 minutes. Add mussels and prawns, reduce heat so liquid barely shimmers and cook 2 minutes. Add salmon and John Dory. Cover and cook 2 minutes. Add scallops. Cover and cook until fish is just translucent and mussels open, about 2 more minutes. As each ingredient is cooked, transfer to platter with vegetables, using slotted spoon.

Bring sauce to simmer in heavy medium saucepan. Mix in chives and spoon over fish. Serve immediately.

❦

Braised Seafood Armorica

*Armorica is the ancient
name for Brittany, where
this dish was created. The
sauce can be prepared well
ahead, then the seafood
added just before serving.
Offer a lightly dressed
salad of chilled romaine
lettuce and mushrooms,
and steaming hot sour-
dough bread and unsalted
butter. Pour a dry California Chenin Blanc or a dry
Sancerre.*

4 to 6 servings

2 tablespoons (¼ stick) butter
1 tablespoon olive oil
6 large shallots, minced
1 garlic clove, minced
1 teaspoon fresh tarragon or
   ¼ teaspoon dried, crumbled
3 tablespoons Cognac
   Generous pinch of
   cayenne pepper
1 cup dry white wine
1 cup Reduced Fish Fumet*
1 cup peeled, seeded, crushed and
   drained tomatoes (about 2 large)
1 tablespoon tomato paste

½ cup whipping cream
   Salt and freshly ground pepper

1 pound large shrimp, shelled and
   deveined (about 12), shells
   reserved for fumet
1½ pounds fish fillets (such as
   haddock, cod, halibut or sea
   bass), cut into ½-inch pieces
2 tablespoons minced fresh parsley

Melt butter with oil in heavy large nonaluminum skillet over medium heat. Add shallot and cook until soft, stirring frequently, 2 to 3 minutes. Blend in garlic and cook 1 minute. Stir in tarragon and cook several seconds. Add Cognac and cayenne pepper and boil until evaporated. Pour in wine and cook until reduced to about 2 tablespoons. Blend in fish fumet, tomatoes and tomato paste and bring to simmer. Reduce heat to low, cover and simmer 30 minutes.

Add cream and cook, uncovered, until reduced to saucelike consistency, about 5 minutes. Season with salt and pepper to taste. Set sauce aside.

About 10 minutes before serving, place sauce over medium-high heat and bring to simmer. Add shrimp and fish and cook until just opaque. Turn into serving dish. Sprinkle top with fresh parsley. Serve immediately.

*Reduced Fish Fumet

Makes 1 cup

2 teaspoons butter
8 ounces fish bones
   Shells from 1 pound shrimp
1 medium onion, thinly sliced
1 small carrot, thinly sliced
¼ to ⅓ cup chopped mushrooms or
   mushroom stems
   (about 2 ounces)

1 bay leaf
10 black peppercorns
   Pinch of dried thyme, crumbled
½ cup dry white wine
3 cups unsalted chicken stock,
   preferably homemade

Melt butter in heavy 4-quart nonaluminum saucepan over low heat. Add fish bones, shrimp shells, onion, carrot, mushrooms, bay leaf, peppercorns and thyme and cook until onion is soft, about 10 minutes. Add wine and bring to boil. Let boil 5 minutes. Add chicken stock and bring to boil. Reduce heat and simmer gently 30 minutes. Strain into large bowl; return liquid to saucepan. Place over high heat and boil until reduced to 1 cup. (*Can be prepared up to 2 months ahead and frozen in airtight container.*)

Fisherman's Stew

A superb party dish courtesy of John Clancy's Restaurant in New York.

6 to 8 servings

Broth
- ½ cup olive oil
- 2 large leeks, sliced (white part only)
- 2 cups coarsely chopped onion
- 3 pounds ripe tomatoes, cored, seeded and coarsely chopped
- 2 cups dry white wine
- ½ cup chopped fresh fennel
- 2 large garlic cloves, crushed
- 1 2- to 3-inch strip orange peel
- 2 bay leaves
- 2 teaspoons salt
- 1 teaspoon dried thyme, crumbled
- 1 large parsley sprig
- ½ teaspoon crushed saffron
- ½ teaspoon freshly ground pepper

Rouille
- 1 large green bell pepper, cored, seeded and chopped
- 1 cup water
- 1 dried red chili or ¼ teaspoon dried red pepper flakes
- ½ cup olive oil
- 4 large garlic cloves
- 2 pimientos
- ¼ cup (or more) dry breadcrumbs

- 2¾ cups Fish Stock*
- 1 1½-pound live lobster
- 1½ pounds halibut, cut into steaks ¾ to 1 inch thick
- 1½ pounds red snapper, cut into fillets ¾ to 1 inch thick
- 1½ pounds bass, cut into steaks ¾ to 1 inch thick
- 1 eel (optional)
- 2 pounds fresh mussels, scrubbed and shucked
- 2 pounds sea scallops
- 12 large French bread croutons

For broth: Heat olive oil in heavy 3-quart saucepan over medium-high heat. Add leeks and onion and sauté until tender, about 7 minutes. Add remaining ingredients and bring to boil. Reduce heat to low, cover and simmer 30 minutes. Strain broth through fine sieve. (*Can be prepared 1 day ahead and refrigerated.*)

For rouille: Bring bell pepper, water and chili to boil in small saucepan over medium heat. Reduce heat to low and simmer until tender, about 10 minutes. Drain well; pat pepper dry. Transfer to blender. Add olive oil, garlic and pimientos and puree until smooth. Turn into serving bowl. Stir in enough breadcrumbs to hold shape on spoon. Set aside. (*Can be prepared 1 day ahead and refrigerated. Bring to room temperature before serving.*)

Bring broth and fish stock to boil in stockpot. Add lobster and boil 5 minutes. Arrange halibut, red snapper, bass and eel over lobster so not completely immersed in broth and boil 5 minutes. Stir in mussels and scallops and boil 5 more minutes. Ladle into heated bowls. Top with croutons and serve. Pass rouille separately.

Vincenzo's Seafood Stew (Zuppa di Frutti di Mare)

Serve this luxurious main-dish stew in large, deep soup bowls.

6 servings

- 2 tablespoons olive oil
- ½ onion, minced
- 1 large garlic clove, minced
- 1 pound cleaned squid, bodies cut into ¼-inch-thick rings
- 1 pound cooked octopus, cut into 1-inch pieces
- 1 pound cuttlefish,* cut into ¼-inch-thick strips
- 1 cup dry white wine
- 4 Italian plum tomatoes, peeled, seeded and diced

- 18 littleneck clams, scrubbed
- 12 jumbo shrimp, unshelled
- 18 mussels, scrubbed and debearded
- 1 pound crayfish or langoustines (optional)
- 18 ½-inch-thick slices French bread, sautéed in olive oil until golden brown
  Salt and freshly ground pepper
  Minced Italian parsley

Heat oil in heavy large saucepan over medium heat. Add onion and cook until light brown, stirring frequently, about 5 minutes. Reduce heat to low. Add garlic and cook 2 minutes, stirring occasionally. Add squid, octopus and cuttlefish. Cook 5 minutes, stirring occasionally. Add wine. Increase heat to medium and cook until liquid is reduced by ⅔, about 25 minutes. Add tomatoes, reduce heat and simmer gently for 10 minutes.

Add clams, shrimp and mussels to soup. Increase heat to medium-high, cover and cook 5 minutes. Add crayfish. Cover and cook until opaque, about 3 minutes. Season with salt and pepper. Place 3 bread slices in each soup bowl. Spoon fish atop bread. Season soup with salt and pepper. Spoon into bowls. Garnish with minced parsley and serve.

*If cuttlefish is unavailable, replace with additional pound of cleaned squid.

*Fish Stock

Makes about 5½ cups

2 pounds fish trimmings (heads, bones, tails), preferably from white fish	1 bay leaf
	3 white peppercorns, crushed
2 medium celery stalks, chopped	½ teaspoon salt
½ cup dry white wine	¼ teaspoon dried thyme, crumbled
1 small leek, chopped (white part only)	

Place fish trimmings in heavy 4-quart saucepan and cover with water. Bring to simmer over medium heat. Cook 5 minutes, skimming foam from surface. Add remaining ingredients, cover partially and continue simmering 30 minutes. Strain mixture through several layers of dampened cheesecloth.

Can be prepared 4 days ahead and refrigerated, or frozen 3 months.

Scallops Florentine

6 servings

3 ounces Parmesan cheese (preferably imported), cut into 3 pieces	1 teaspoon freshly grated nutmeg
	½ teaspoon freshly ground white pepper
3 large garlic cloves	1¼ pounds bay scallops, rinsed and drained
1¼ pounds fresh spinach, dried thoroughly, stems cut off and reserved	8 ounces shell or other small pasta, cooked al dente and drained

½ cup (1 stick) unsalted butter
1 teaspoon salt
1 cup whipping cream

Position rack in center of oven and preheat to 425°F.

Chop Parmesan finely in processor. Set aside. With machine running, drop garlic through feed tube and mince finely. Add spinach stems and mince.

Melt butter in heavy 12-inch skillet over medium-low heat. Stir in garlic mixture and sauté until stems are very soft, about 8 minutes. Add whipping cream and simmer until reduced by half, about 5 minutes.

Coarsely chop spinach leaves in processor in batches using on/off turns. Add to cream mixture with nutmeg and pepper. Increase heat to high and cook until spinach is heated through, about 3 minutes. Remove from heat. Stir in scallops and pasta. Transfer to shallow 4-quart baking dish. Sprinkle reserved Parmesan cheese over top. Bake until scallops are just opaque, about 10 to 12 minutes. Serve immediately.

Ginger Shrimp with Pea Pods

4 servings

2 tablespoons vegetable or peanut oil
¼ teaspoon oriental sesame oil or to taste
12 ounces medium shrimp, shelled and deveined
1 garlic clove, crushed
1½ cups fresh or frozen snow peas (about 4 ounces)

1 8-pound can sliced water chestnuts, drained
½ cup chicken stock
2 tablespoons soy sauce or to taste
1 tablespoon cornstarch
1 tablespoon cold water
1 tablespoon grated fresh ginger
Chow mein noodles or freshly cooked rice

Heat oils in wok or heavy skillet until hot but not smoking. Add shrimp and stir-fry 2 minutes. Transfer to plate and set aside. Add garlic to wok and stir 15 to 20 seconds. Add snow peas, water chestnuts, stock and soy sauce and stir-fry 2 minutes. Combine cornstarch and water in small cup and blend until smooth. Add to wok. Return shrimp to wok with ginger and stir until sauce thickens and mixture is heated through. Serve immediately over chow mein noodles or rice.

Shrimp and Sweet Peppers

A Tunisian sauté accompanied by fiery Harissa sauce.

4 servings

2 garlic cloves, minced
2 teaspoons ground coriander
2 tablespoons olive oil
1 large green bell pepper, cored, seeded and thinly sliced
1 large red bell pepper, cored, seeded and thinly sliced
8 ounces medium shrimp, peeled and deveined

2 tablespoons tomato paste
½ teaspoon salt
½ teaspoon freshly ground pepper
½ cup water
1 egg, beaten to blend
Harissa (see page 112)
Chopped green onion
Lemon wedges

Mix garlic and coriander. Heat oil in heavy medium skillet over medium heat. Add peppers and sauté 1 minute. Stir in garlic mixture and shrimp. Blend in tomato paste, salt and pepper. Add water and simmer gently 4 minutes. Pour egg over surface. Shake pan to integrate egg and thicken sauce. Turn into bowl. Serve with harissa, green onion and lemon wedges.

7 🍎 Poultry

It is not surprising that Americans are eating more poultry every year: It is inexpensive, extraordinarily versatile, and low in fat and calories. And because poultry makes such a perfect foil for more assertively flavored ingredients, it is a natural for one-dish meals.

Poultry lends itself to myriad cooking methods, both in the oven and on the range, and this selection is representative. For a quick skillet supper choose Chicken-Artichoke-Mushroom Sauté (page 78) or Italian Stir-fried Chicken (page 80). Stovetop braises such as Cecile van Lanschot's Chicken with Currants and Green Peppercorns (page 79) and Chicken Hardeman (page 80), take only a few minutes more, while for long, leisurely simmering you might try La Poule au Pot du Bon Roy Henry (page 82) and Guatemalan Duck Stew with Potatoes (page 87). And then there are the oven-braised dishes—Baked Mediterranean Chicken (page 78), Provençal Chicken, zesty Basque Chicken (both on page 81), and Poulet à la Bonne Femme (page 82)—as well as a medley of juicy casserole-roasted combinations.

With this assortment of recipes, "a chicken in every pot" is just the beginning. Extend the *batterie de cuisine* to skillets and casseroles, roasting pans and *cocottes* . . . and the possibilities for delectable one-dish dinners are almost limitless.

Chicken-Artichoke-Mushroom Sauté

Veal scallops may be used in place of chicken breasts.

4 servings

2 large chicken breasts, boned, skinned and halved
All purpose flour
Butter
8 to 10 mushrooms, sliced
1 15-ounce can artichoke hearts, rinsed and well drained

½ cup chicken stock
¼ cup white wine
Juice of ½ lemon or to taste
Salt and freshly ground pepper

Dredge chicken with flour; shake off excess. Melt butter in medium skillet, add chicken and sauté until golden brown and cooked through. Transfer to heated platter. Add mushrooms to skillet and sauté 1 to 2 minutes. Stir in artichoke hearts, stock, wine, lemon juice and salt and pepper to taste and let cook until sauce is reduced slightly, stirring occasionally. Return chicken to skillet and warm through. Serve immediately.

Baked Mediterranean Chicken

6 servings

½ cup fresh parsley leaves

Marinade
2 large garlic cloves
½ cup olive oil
¼ cup safflower oil
2 teaspoons dried oregano, crumbled
2 teaspoons ground coriander
2 teaspoons salt
1 teaspoon dried red pepper flakes
Freshly ground pepper

3 medium lemons, ends cut flat

2 medium-size red bell peppers, cut into 2-inch rectangles
2 3-pound chickens, cut into serving pieces
1 10-ounce package frozen artichoke hearts, thawed and drained
10 ounces pearl onions, peeled
10 large black olives (preferably Kalamata)

½ teaspoon salt
Freshly ground pepper

Finely mince parsley in food processor. Remove from work bowl and set aside.

For marinade: With machine running, drop garlic through processor feed tube and mince finely. Add olive oil, safflower oil, oregano, coriander, salt, red pepper flakes and pepper and blend 2 seconds. Transfer marinade to heavy-duty large plastic bag.

Insert medium slicer into processor. Stand 1 lemon in feed tube and slice using firm pressure. Repeat with remaining lemons. Reserve 6 slices. Add remainder to marinade. Stand red bell pepper rectangles in feed tube lengthwise, packing tightly. Slice into matchsticks using light pressure. Add to marinade with chicken pieces, artichoke hearts, pearl onions and olives. Marinate mixture at room temperature for 2 hours, turning bag occasionally.

Position rack in center of oven and preheat to 475°F. Arrange chicken skin side down in single layer in 18-inch oval baking dish. Add onions (set aside remaining vegetables and marinade). Season with ¼ teaspoon salt and pepper. Bake 30 minutes. Turn chicken and stir onions. Season with remaining ¼ teaspoon salt and pepper. Continue baking until chicken is tender, about 10 to 15 minutes.

Remove bell pepper, artichoke hearts and olives from marinade and arrange over chicken. Discard marinade. Bake until juices run clear when chicken is pricked with fork, about 5 minutes. Degrease cooking juices, then spoon over chicken and vegetables. Garnish with reserved lemon slices and minced parsley and serve immediately.

Cecile van Lanschot's Chicken with Currants and Green Peppercorns

This recipe, created by a Dutch cookbook author, is an elegant do-ahead dish for a dinner party or special family gathering. Serve with hot buttered fettuccine tossed with chopped fresh parsley and a robust red wine such as a Cabernet Sauvignon or Bordeaux.

4 to 5 servings

1½ tablespoons butter
1 tablespoon olive oil
1 3-pound chicken, cut into 8 pieces and all pieces except wings skinned
1 pound small boiling onions (about 1 inch in diameter), peeled
½ cup rich chicken stock, preferably homemade
2 ounces dried currants (about 5 tablespoons)

1 tablespoon water-packed green peppercorns, drained and lightly crushed (or to taste)
Salt
1½ cups seedless grapes (about 8 ounces)
¼ cup dry white wine

¼ cup whipping cream
1 to 1½ tablespoons Dijon or green peppercorn mustard
Salt and freshly ground pepper

Heat butter and oil in heavy large nonaluminum skillet over medium-high heat. Add chicken in batches (do not crowd) and cook until browned on all sides, about 10 minutes. Remove chicken. Add onions to skillet and cook until just beginning to brown, about 2 minutes. Add stock, currants and green peppercorns and stir, scraping up any browned bits. Return chicken to skillet. Season lightly with salt if desired. Place over medium-high heat and bring to simmer. Reduce heat, cover partially and cook until barely tender, about 20 minutes. Meanwhile, combine grapes and wine in medium saucepan over medium heat and simmer gently about 3 minutes. Set aside. (*Dish can be prepared 1 to 2 days ahead to this point and refrigerated. Skim fat from braising liquid and reheat chicken slowly before continuing with recipe.*)

Add cream, mustard and grape mixture to chicken. Increase heat to medium-high and simmer until sauce is slightly thickened, stirring carefully so grapes do not break up. Taste and adjust seasoning with salt and pepper. Transfer chicken to heated platter. Arrange grapes and onions around chicken using slotted spoon. Pour sauce over. Serve immediately.

Fried Corncakes with Chicken, Mussels and Saffron

A whole meal on one plate—and a beautiful presentation.

4 servings

2 cups water
2 tablespoons (¼ stick) unsalted butter
½ cup yellow cornmeal

1 cup dry white wine
24 mussels, scrubbed and debearded

Pinch of saffron threads, crushed
¾ cup whipping cream
¼ teaspoon minced garlic
¼ teaspoon minced shallot

6 skinned and boned chicken breast halves, each cut lengthwise into 4 strips
2 medium-large zucchini, halved crosswise and cut into julienne
2 large carrots, halved crosswise and cut into julienne
8 ounces snow peas, cut into julienne
Salt and freshly ground pepper

Generously butter 9-inch square pan. Bring water and 1 tablespoon butter to boil in heavy medium saucepan. Gradually add cornmeal and cook until beginning to bubble, stirring constantly. Reduce heat to low and stir until mixture is thick and begins to pull away from sides of pan, about 25 minutes. Pour into prepared pan, spreading evenly. Cool mixture completely.

Meanwhile, bring wine to boil in large skillet. Add mussels. Cover and cook until mussels open, 3 to 4 minutes, shaking pan occasionally. Remove opened mussels. Cook unopened mussels for 3 more minutes. Discard any remaining unopened mussels. Set mussels aside. Strain liquid through sieve lined with several layers of dampened cheesecloth. Return to skillet, boil until reduced to ¼ cup.

Cut cornmeal into 12 to 16 "cakes" using 1¾- to 2-inch fluted round cutter. Melt remaining 1 tablespoon butter in heavy medium skillet over medium heat. Add corncakes (in batches if necessary; do not crowd) and fry until crisp and golden brown, turning once, 7 to 8 minutes. Cover and keep warm.

Dissolve saffron in 1 tablespoon mussel liquid. Stir back into liquid. Add cream, garlic and shallot and cook over medium-high heat until slightly thickened, about 5 minutes. Add chicken and cook until just firm, about 3 minutes. Remove chicken from sauce. Add vegetables. Season with salt and pepper. Cook until vegetables are crisp-tender and sauce is thick enough to coat back of spoon.

Alternate chicken strips and mussels around edge of each plate. Place corncakes in center. Using tongs, arrange vegetables over chicken. Spoon sauce over corncakes and serve.

Chicken Hardeman

This colorful main course is perfect for entertaining because much of the preparation can be done in advance.

4 servings

¼ cup olive oil
1 2½- to 3-pound frying chicken, cut up
1 large onion, chopped
⅓ cup chopped fresh parsley
1 teaspoon dried basil, crumbled
1 garlic clove, crushed
¼ cup dry Sherry
1 teaspoon salt

¼ teaspoon freshly ground pepper
1 16-ounce can whole tomatoes, drained and chopped (reserve juice)
8 ounces mushrooms, thinly sliced
½ cup pitted ripe olives, sliced

Parsley sprigs

Heat olive oil in large skillet over medium-high heat. Add chicken pieces and brown on all sides. Set chicken aside. Add onion, parsley, basil and garlic to skillet. Reduce heat to medium-low, cover and cook until onion is soft, about 10 minutes, stirring occasionally. Add Sherry. Increase heat to high and simmer, uncovered, until liquid evaporates, about 2 minutes. Season with salt and pepper. Add chopped tomato and juice, mushrooms and olives and stir through. Arrange reserved chicken pieces and juices on top of onion mixture. (*Recipe can be prepared ahead to this point and refrigerated.*) Reduce heat to medium-low. Cover and simmer until chicken is tender and cooked through, about 25 to 35 minutes.

Transfer chicken to heated serving platter using slotted spoon. Degrease sauce in skillet if necessary. Increase heat to high and boil sauce until reduced and thickened, about 5 minutes. Spoon sauce over chicken. Garnish with parsley sprigs. Serve immediately.

Italian Stir-fried Chicken

4 servings

3 tablespoons olive oil
1 garlic clove, minced
2 whole large chicken breasts, skinned, boned and cut into 1-inch squares
1 cup fresh or thawed frozen Italian green beans
½ cup chopped red bell pepper
¼ cup chopped green onion (white part only)

½ teaspoon salt
4 medium tomatoes, quartered
4 anchovies, mashed to a paste
2 tablespoons diced pimiento
1 tablespoon capers, rinsed and drained
1 to 2 tablespoons fresh lemon juice
1 teaspoon cayenne pepper or to taste

Place wok or large skillet over high heat until very hot, about 30 seconds. Add oil and garlic and stir fry 10 seconds. Add chicken, beans, chopped red bell pepper, onion and salt and continue stirring until chicken is cooked through, about 3 minutes. Add tomatoes, anchovies, pimiento and capers and stir-fry 1 minute. Sprinkle with lemon juice and toss through. Turn onto heated platter, sprinkle with cayenne and serve.

Provençal Chicken

This dish can be prepared up to three months ahead and frozen. Thaw before baking.

6 to 8 servings

2 tablespoons (¼ stick) butter
8 ounces mushrooms, sliced

4 whole chicken breasts, quartered
2 large onions, sliced
1 tablespoon all purpose flour

2 garlic cloves, crushed
1 small bay leaf
¼ cup chopped fresh parsley

½ teaspoon dried thyme, crumbled or 1 teaspoon minced fresh
⅛ teaspoon dried fennel greens, crumbled
8 saffron threads dissolved in 3 tablespoons water
Grated peel and juice of 1 orange
2 cups peeled fresh tomatoes
½ cup dry white wine

Melt 1 tablespoon butter in large skillet over medium heat. Add sliced mushrooms and sauté until just tender, about 3 to 4 minutes. Set mushrooms aside.

Preheat oven to 350°F. Melt remaining 1 tablespoon butter in another large skillet over medium heat. Add chicken and brown on all sides. Add onion and cook until soft, about 5 minutes. Sprinkle flour over chicken and mix well. Transfer chicken to 3-quart baking dish using tongs. Top with reserved mushrooms. Set baking dish aside.

Add garlic, bay leaf, parsley, thyme, fennel and saffron threads to skillet with orange peel. Cook over medium heat 3 to 4 minutes, stirring constantly. Add orange juice, tomatoes and wine. Increase heat to high and bring to boil, stirring constantly. Pour over chicken and mushrooms. Cover and bake until chicken is tender, about 45 minutes. Serve immediately.

Basque Chicken

4 to 6 servings

1 cup all purpose flour
½ teaspoon salt
¼ teaspoon freshly ground pepper
1 2½- to 3½-pound frying chicken, cut into 6 pieces
¼ cup olive oil
4 large tomatoes, peeled, seeded and chopped

4 ounces lean ham, diced
1 4-ounce jar pimientos, drained and sliced, *or* 1 small roasted red bell pepper, peeled, seeded and chopped
½ cup dry white wine
Chopped fresh parsley
Freshly cooked rice (optional)

Preheat oven to 350°F. Combine flour, salt and pepper in medium bowl. Dredge chicken pieces in flour mixture, shaking off excess. Heat oil in large skillet over medium heat. Add chicken pieces and brown on all sides. Transfer to 3- or 4-quart baking dish with tight-fitting lid (or set aside to return to skillet for stovetop cooking). Drain oil from skillet. Add tomatoes and ham and cook over medium heat, stirring frequently, 5 minutes. Stir in pimientos. Add wine and simmer 3 to 4 minutes. Pour over chicken in dish (or return chicken to skillet). Cover and bake (or cook over low heat) until chicken is cooked through, about 25 minutes. Sprinkle with chopped parsley and serve immediately over rice.

Poulet à la Bonne Femme

*A Louisiana version of
the French classic.*

8 servings

4 whole chicken breasts, halved,
  patted dry
8 chicken legs, patted dry
8 large baking potatoes, unpeeled,
  each cut lengthwise into
  ½-inch-thick slices, patted dry
  Salt and freshly ground pepper
1 pound sliced bacon

¼ cup all purpose flour
4 cups chicken stock

1 tablespoon chopped fresh thyme
  or 1 teaspoon dried, crumbled
1 tablespoon chopped fresh
  marjoram or 1 teaspoon dried,
  crumbled

1½ teaspoons chopped fresh sage or
  ½ teaspoon dried, crumbled
1½ teaspoons chopped fresh
  rosemary or ½ teaspoon dried,
  crumbled
1 teaspoon salt
½ teaspoon freshly ground pepper
½ teaspoon cayenne pepper
¼ teaspoon freshly grated nutmeg
5 onions, halved and thinly sliced
1 bunch green onions, sliced
¼ cup minced fresh parsley

Season chicken and potatoes with salt and pepper. Cook bacon in heavy large skillet over medium-high heat until crisp. Drain on paper towels. Add chicken to same skillet in batches in single layer and brown in hot bacon drippings until golden, 2 to 3 minutes per side. Drain chicken on paper towels.

Arrange potato slices in single layer in same skillet over medium heat and cook until well browned, about 4 minutes per side, turning carefully. Drain potato slices on paper towels.

Discard all but 4 tablespoons bacon drippings from skillet. Reheat remainder over medium heat. Remove from heat and stir in flour. Return to heat and stir until roux begins to brown, 4 to 5 minutes. Stir in stock. Increase heat and bring to boil. Reduce heat to low and simmer until thickened.

Preheat oven to 350°F. Blend seasonings in small bowl. Arrange 4 chicken breasts and 4 drumsticks alternately in 10-inch baking dish. Cover with layer of browned potato slices. Cover with half of sliced onions. Sprinkle with half of seasoning mixture. Add layer of bacon. Repeat layering with remaining chicken, potato slices, onions, seasoning mixture and bacon. Sprinkle with green onions and parsley. Pour reserved sauce into dish. Cover and bake 30 minutes. Uncover and continue baking 15 minutes. Serve immediately.

La Poule au Pot du Bon Roy Henry

8 servings

1 pound onions, halved

1 6-pound chicken, legs and wings
  tied to body with string
5 quarts (about) chicken stock
6 leeks
2 pounds carrots
2 pounds turnips
4 celery stalks

3 tomatoes, chopped
  Bouquet garni (1 fresh thyme
  sprig or ¼ teaspoon dried,
  crumbled, 1 bay leaf)
1 tablespoon freshly ground pepper
1 teaspoon ground cloves

Boudin*
Salt and freshly ground pepper

Heat heavy large skillet over high heat. Add onions and cook until charred.

Place chicken in Dutch oven. Add enough stock to cover. Boil 15 minutes, skimming surface frequently. Cut 3 leeks, 1 pound carrots, 1 pound turnips and 2 celery stalks into 1-inch pieces. Add to chicken with onions, tomatoes, bouquet garni, pepper and cloves. Simmer until chicken is very tender, about 1½ hours.

Remove chicken from broth using slotted spoon. Cut into 8 pieces. Strain broth through sieve lined with several layers of cheesecloth; return to pot.

Peel remaining carrots and turnips and cut into 1-inch pieces; round edges with paring knife. Add to broth. Simmer 10 minutes. Cut remaining leeks and celery stalks into 2-inch strips ½ inch wide. Add to broth. Simmer until vegetables are tender, about 10 minutes. Return chicken to pot. Add boudin. Simmer until heated through. Season with salt and pepper.

---

*Boudin

Makes about 10

1 6-foot sausage casing
3 tablespoons distilled white vinegar

2 ounces chicken livers
2 tablespoons Port
1 garlic clove, minced

12 ounces boned and skinned chicken breast, cut into 1-inch cubes
3 shallots
3 garlic cloves

1 egg
1 egg yolk
⅔ cup crème fraîche
½ teaspoon salt
¼ teaspoon freshly ground pepper
½ cup minced fresh parsley

3 cups chicken stock
Bouquet garni (2 fresh thyme sprigs or ½ teaspoon dried, crumbled, 1 bay leaf)
10 whole peppercorns

Soak casing in cold water with vinegar 1 hour. Rinse. Slip 1 end of casing over faucet and run cold water through. Clip or tie closed any section with holes. Soak in fresh cold water.

Combine livers, Port and minced garlic in small bowl. Marinate livers 1 hour, turning occasionally.

Finely chop chicken, shallots and 3 garlic cloves in processor. With machine running, add egg and yolk through feed tube, then add crème fraîche in thin stream and blend. Add livers with marinade and salt and pepper. Puree until smooth. Mix in parsley. Refrigerate at least 30 minutes. (*Can be prepared 1 day ahead to this point.*)

Attach stuffing horn to meat grinder. Wring out casing and place one end over horn. Gradually push all of casing onto horn, leaving 6-inch overhang. Tie knot in overhang. With right hand, feed meat mixture into grinder. Meanwhile, anchor casing atop horn with left thumb, allowing casing to unroll as mixture is extruded. Stop occasionally to mold meat. Do not pack too full or sausage will burst as filling expands during cooking. Remove horn and knot casing. (Casing can also be stuffed with pastry bag fitted with ½-inch plain tip.)

To form individual sausages, knot 3-inch-long pieces of string around casing at 4-inch intervals.

Place sausages in shallow pan. Bring stock to boil with bouquet garni and peppercorns. Pour over sausage. Weight with plate. Cover pan and let stand 45 minutes, turning sausages once. Cut into individual sausages. (*Can be prepared 1 day ahead. Wrap sausages tightly and refrigerate.*)

My Own Chicken

This recipe is from French chef Michel Guérard.

4 servings

1 3- to 3½-pound chicken, cut up and patted dry
⅓ cup dry vermouth
8 baby carrots, peeled and trimmed, or 2 large carrots cut into eight 2-inch strips
8 baby leeks (white part only) or 8 green onions (white and light green parts only)
8 pearl or boiling onions, parboiled and peeled
4 baby turnips, or 1 large turnip cut into four 2-inch strips

4 fresh parsley sprigs
2 fresh thyme sprigs or 1 teaspoon dried, crumbled
1 large bay leaf
2½ cups whipping cream

2 tablespoons minced fresh chervil, tarragon or thyme
   Salt and freshly ground white pepper

Arrange chicken legs, thighs and backs (if using) in single layer in deep heavy skillet or saucepan. Pour vermouth over. Add carrots, leeks, onions, turnips, parsley, thyme and bay leaf. Beat cream until soft peaks form. Pour over chicken and vegetables. Bring to simmer over medium heat. Cover partially and simmer 5 minutes, adjusting heat so liquid is just shaking. Add chicken breast halves and wings, pushing down into liquid. Continue simmering until chicken is opaque, 20 to 25 minutes; do not overcook.

Remove chicken and vegetables to large strainer. Discard parsley, thyme and bay leaf. Cover chicken with foil. Degrease cooking liquid. Clean skillet; return cooking liquid to skillet. Add 1 tablespoon minced fresh herbs and boiling onions if not cooked through. Boil until liquid thickens and reduces to about 1¼ cups. Season with salt and freshly ground white pepper.

Arrange chicken and vegetables on platter. Season with salt and white pepper. Spoon sauce over. Sprinkle with remaining 1 tablespoon minced fresh herbs. Serve immediately.

Saffron Chicken Fricassee with Dumplings

2 servings

1 whole chicken breast, skinned, boned and cut into thin strips
   Salt and freshly ground pepper

1 tablespoon cornstarch
1 tablespoon vegetable oil

1 egg white

2 cups chicken stock

2 tablespoons (¼ stick) butter
¼ cup chopped onion
¼ cup sliced celery
¼ cup sliced carrot
¼ cup dry white wine

2 tablespoons minced fresh parsley
2 tablespoons snipped fresh chives
⅛ teaspoon powdered saffron

½ cup all purpose flour
¾ teaspoon baking powder
¼ teaspoon salt
¼ cup (about) milk

1 tablespoon cornstarch dissolved in 1 tablespoon water
¼ cup whipping cream
   Minced fresh parsley (garnish)

Pat chicken dry. Arrange in dish. Sprinkle with salt and pepper. Let stand at room temperature 20 minutes.

Sprinkle chicken with 1 tablespoon cornstarch and oil. Let stand at room temperature 20 minutes.

Fold egg white into chicken. Let stand at room temperature 20 minutes.

Bring stock to simmer in large saucepan. Add chicken and simmer 2 minutes. Remove using slotted spoon. Boil broth until reduced to 1¼ cups.

Melt 1 tablespoon butter in heavy large saucepan over medium-low heat. Add onion, celery and carrot and stir until slightly softened, about 5 minutes. Add reduced broth, wine, 2 tablespoons parsley, 1 tablespoon chives and saffron and bring to simmer. Cover and cook until vegetables are tender, about 10 minutes.

Meanwhile, combine flour, remaining chives, baking powder and ¼ teaspoon salt in medium bowl. Cut in remaining butter until mixture resembles coarse meal. Stir in enough milk to make firm batter that can be dropped from spoon.

Stir dissolved cornstarch into simmering broth in slow stream. Stir in cream. Drop batter into broth by heaping tablespoonfuls. Cover and cook 12 minutes. Transfer dumplings to soup plates using slotted spoon. Return chicken to broth and heat through. Season with salt and pepper. Ladle fricassee over dumplings. Garnish with parsley. Serve immediately.

Roast Chicken Stuffed with Pasta

This recipe can be doubled.

2 servings

1 ounce dried mushrooms
¼ cup boiling water

2½ tablespoons unsalted butter
1 to 2 chicken livers, trimmed and patted dry
Pinch *each* of dried thyme and cayenne pepper

2 ounces fresh mushrooms, cut into matchstick julienne
1 medium-size red bell pepper, cut into matchstick julienne

2 ounces baked ham, finely chopped
2 tablespoons chopped fresh Italian parsley

3 ounces fresh fettuccine or 2 ounces dried
Salt and freshly ground pepper

1 2½- to 3-pound chicken
Olive oil

Soak mushrooms in boiling water until soft, about 15 minutes. Drain, reserving liquid. Rinse and drain again. Discard hard stems; chop caps.

Melt 1 tablespoon butter in heavy medium skillet over medium-high heat. Add livers, thyme and cayenne and cook until livers are brown outside but still pink inside, turning once, 5 minutes. Chop coarsely and transfer to large bowl.

Melt remaining 1½ tablespoons butter in same skillet over medium-high heat. Add fresh mushrooms and red bell pepper and sauté until mushroom liquid evaporates. Add to livers with dried mushrooms, ham and parsley.

Cook fettuccine in boiling salted water until al dente (firm to bite). Drain well. Toss with liver mixture. Season with salt and freshly ground pepper.

Preheat oven to 400°F. Pat chicken dry. Rub inside and out with salt and pepper. Fill chicken with fettuccine, packing in as much as possible without compressing (bake any extra mixture, covered, 20 to 25 minutes). Truss chicken tightly, closing cavities. Place in small roasting pan. Brush lightly with olive oil. Roast until juices run clear when thigh is pierced with knife tip, basting occasionally, about 50 minutes. Let stand 5 minutes. Cut chicken in half with poultry shears. Set each half on plate stuffing side up. Serve immediately.

For variation, spoon pasta onto serving platter and set chicken on top of pasta skin side up.

Basic Chicken en Cocotte

The following two recipes also refer to this basic en cocotte *technique.*

4 servings

1 3½-pound chicken, room temperature
Salt and freshly ground pepper

2 tablespoons vegetable oil
1 tablespoon butter

Preheat oven to 400°F. Remove neck and giblets from chicken. Discard loose fat from cavity. Cut off tail and wing tips. Pat chicken dry. Truss chicken if desired. Sprinkle with salt and pepper. Heat oil and butter in heavy 5-quart oval casserole over medium-high heat. Place chicken in pan on its side. Cover pan with large spatter screen if desired. Cook first side until brown. (If fat begins to turn dark brown at any time, reduce heat to medium.) Using 2 wooden spoons, gently turn chicken onto breast and cook until brown. Turn chicken onto second side and cook until brown. Turn chicken breast side up and cook until back is light brown. Baste chicken with pan juices.

Cover casserole, transfer to oven and bake chicken until juices run clear when pierced in thickest part of leg with thin skewer, about 45 minutes. (If juices are still pink, bake several minuters longer and test again.) Transfer chicken to platter. Discard trussing strings, if used. Degrease pan juices and bring to boil. Adjust seasoning. (*Chicken can be tented with foil and kept warm in turned-off oven 20 minutes.*) Serve chicken, passing juices separately.

Variations

For Cornish game hens: Use two 1½-pound hens. Brown hens as above. Bake until juices from cavity run clear when hens are lifted, 35 minutes.

For squab: Use four 12- to 14-ounce squab. Brown 2 minutes per side, propping against sides of casserole if necessary to hold in place. Bake until juices from cavity run clear when squab are lifted, about 30 minutes.

Chicken with Potatoes, Leeks and Dill

4 servings

1 3½-pound chicken, room temperature
Salt and freshly ground pepper
2 tablespoons vegetable oil
1 tablespoon unsalted butter

1½ pounds boiling potatoes, peeled and cut into 1½-inch pieces

2 fresh dill sprigs

2 large leeks (white and light green parts only), cut into 2 × ¼-inch pieces

2 tablespoons dry white wine
½ cup whipping cream
2 tablespoons minced fresh dill

Cook chicken as in Basic Chicken en Cocotte (see previous recipe), using 2 tablespoons vegetable oil and 1 tablespoon butter to brown chicken.

Meanwhile, cover potatoes with water in large saucepan and bring to boil. Add salt. Reduce heat, cover and simmer until almost tender, about 15 minutes. Drain thoroughly.

When chicken is finished baking, transfer to platter, reserving pan juices. Tent chicken with foil.

Bring pan juices to boil. Add potatoes and dill sprigs; season with salt and pepper. Reduce heat and simmer until potatoes are light brown and just tender, turning frequently, about 10 minutes. Transfer potatoes to bowl using slotted spoon; keep warm. Discard dill. Reserve pan juices.

Add leeks to casserole; season with salt and pepper. Cover and cook over low heat until tender, stirring occasionally, about 10 minutes. Discard any juices on platter. Arrange leeks around chicken using slotted spoon. Reserve pan juices in casserole. Arrange potatoes atop leeks. Tent with foil.

Degrease pan juices and bring to boil. Add wine and return to boil, scraping up any browned bits on bottom and sides of casserole. Add cream and bring to boil, stirring constantly. Reduce heat and simmer until sauce thickens and coats back of spoon, stirring frequently, about 3 minutes. Strain into sauce dish. Sprinkle potatoes with 1 teaspoon minced dill; stir remaining dill into sauce. Adjust seasoning. Serve chicken immediately, passing sauce separately.

Chicken with Rosemary and Zucchini

4 servings

1 3½-pound chicken
Salt and freshly ground pepper
3 tablespoons olive oil

4 garlic cloves, minced
2 tablespoons minced fresh rosemary or 2 teaspoons dried, crumbled

3 medium zucchini, cut into 2 × ¼-inch strips

⅓ cup dry white wine

Cook chicken as in Basic Chicken en Cocotte (see page 86), using 3 tablespoons olive oil to brown.

Five minutes before chicken is finished baking, stir garlic and 1 tablespoon rosemary into pan juices. Baste chicken and cover. Reduce oven temperature to 350°F and continue baking 5 more minutes. Transfer chicken to platter, reserving pan juices. Tent chicken with foil to keep warm.

Bring pan juices to boil over medium heat. Add zucchini and season with salt and pepper. Cook, stirring occasionally, until crisp-tender, about 3 minutes. Discard any juices on platter. Arrange zucchini around chicken using slotted spoon. Tent with foil. Reserve pan juices in casserole.

Degrease pan juices and bring to boil. Add wine and return to boil, skimming fat frequently and scraping up any browned bits on bottom and sides of casserole. Boil until thickened slightly, about 2 minutes. Add remaining 1 tablespoon rosemary. Reduce heat and simmer 2 minutes, stirring frequently. Adjust seasoning. Serve immediately, passing sauce separately.

Duck Stew with Potatoes (Pato Guisado)

From the Caribbean coast of Guatemala.

3 to 4 servings

4 cups water
1 4½-pound duck, cut into serving pieces, loose skin and fat discarded
2 tablespoons cider vinegar
1 teaspoon salt

1½ cups peeled and chopped fresh or canned tomatoes
1 cup chicken stock
1 onion, sliced

6 garlic cloves, sliced
6 bay leaves
1½ teaspoons dried thyme, crumbled
¾ teaspoon dried oregano, crumbled
1½ teaspoons vegetable oil
¾ teaspoon annatto (achiote) seeds*

3 cups peeled ½-inch potato cubes
Cooked rice
Tortillas

Combine water, duck, vinegar and 1 teaspoon salt in heavy large saucepan. Bring to boil, skimming surface. Reduce heat and simmer 15 minutes. Drain duck and return to saucepan.

Puree tomatoes with stock, onion and garlic in processor. Add to duck. Stir in bay leaves, thyme and oregano. Season with salt. Heat oil in heavy small skillet over low heat. Add annatto and stir until oil is orange, about 3 minutes. Strain over duck. Bring mixture to boil. Reduce heat, cover and simmer 1 hour, turning duck occasionally.

Add potatoes to stew. Cover and cook until duck and potatoes are tender, about 15 minutes. (*Can be prepared 1 day ahead and refrigerated. Discard fat before rewarming.*) Degrease sauce. Adjust seasoning. Discard bay leaves. Serve stew with rice and tortillas.

*Available at Latin American markets.

Jerry Friedman

Fried Corncakes
with Chicken,
Mussels and
Saffron

Charcuterie Salad

*Lemon Fish with Vegetables
and Parsley Sauce*

Roast Chicken Stuffed with Pasta

Dan Wolfe

Clockwise from top left:
Karelian Rice and Rye Pasties with Egg
Butter; Iron Miner's Pasties; Helsinki
Vegetable Pie; Carrot Pie

Ragout of Pork Catalan

8 ❧ Meat

A quick, light stir-fry . . . a robust, long-cooking stew . . . zesty chili. These are only a sampling of the countless choices among one-dish entrées made with meat. True, we are eating more poultry and seafood nowadays; but for must of us, beef, pork and lamb are continuing favorites for family and company meals alike.

And Americans are hardly alone in their enthusiasm for meat dishes; in fact, most of the recipes in this chapter have their roots in the cooking of other lands. Stir-fries like Broccoli Beef (page 91) and Hot Garlic Eggplant with pork (page 100) usually look to the East. Braises and stews are more typically of Occidental inspiration, and it seems that nearly every European cuisine has made a contribution: Belgian Carbonnade Flamande (page 92), German Hunter's One-Pot (page 93), Greek Stifado (page 113), Hungarian Sauerkraut and Pork Gulyás with Sour Cream (page 101), Italian Braised Oxtails with Gremolata (page 94), Portuguese Braised Lamb in Red Wine Sauce (page 111), Russian Cholent (page 94), Spanish Ragout of Pork Catalan (page 102)—not to mention such regional specialties as Provençal Ratatouille with Sausage (page 103), Alsatian Baeckaoffa (page 95), and Bosnian Hot Pot (page 110).

That they enjoy such global popularity is surely the best compliment to these one-dish meat dinners. They are all inventive and richly satisfying, and they rarely demand to-the-minute timing. In short, they represent home cooking at its best.

🍎 *Beef and Veal*

Crazy Mary's Chili

The presentation of this chili—topped with a layer of melted cheese and a spoonful of sour cream—is very attractive.

6 to 8 servings

2 tablespoons chili powder
1 teaspoon salt
½ teaspoon freshly ground pepper
¼ cup (½ stick) butter or margarine
2 cups sliced mushrooms
    (7 to 8 large)
1 cup chopped onion
1 cup chopped celery
1 pound lean ground beef
2 28-ounce cans crushed tomatoes
    packed in puree

¼ cup water
1 tablespoon sugar
1 teaspoon Worcestershire sauce
2 cups canned kidney beans,
    drained

Shredded cheddar cheese
Sour cream

Combine chili powder, salt and pepper in cup; set aside. Melt butter in heavy large saucepan over medium heat. Add mushrooms, onion and celery and cook, stirring occasionally, until onion is transparent, about 10 minutes. Add ground beef and about ¼ of chili powder mixture. Cook, breaking up meat with fork, until browned. Stir in remaining chili powder mixture, tomatoes, water, sugar and Worcestershire. Cover partially and simmer 15 minutes. Add beans and simmer 10 more minutes.

Ladle chili into broilerproof serving bowls. Sprinkle each serving with about 2 tablespoons shredded cheddar cheese. Broil just until cheese melts. Top each with dollop of sour cream. Serve immediately.

Lahanodolmades (Stuffed Cabbage)

6 to 8 servings

2 medium heads of cabbage

2 tablespoons olive oil
2 large onions, chopped
1 pound ground beef or lamb
1 garlic clove, finely chopped
⅛ teaspoon cinnamon
    Salt and freshly ground pepper
2 tablespoons tomato paste

⅓ cup uncooked rice
1½ cups (or more) tomato sauce,
    preferably homemade
½ cup beef stock
¼ cup toasted pine nuts

1 tablespoon butter, cut into pieces
    Lemon slices or Greek Lemon
    Sauce*

Carefully remove outer cabbage leaves without tearing. (Reserve remaining cabbage for another use.) Bring large amount of water to boil in saucepan. Add cabbage leaves and cook until just tender, about 5 minutes. Drain and let cool slightly. Trim heavy veins in centers using paring knife, being careful not to cut leaves. Cut each leaf in half lengthwise. Set aside.

Heat olive oil in large skillet over medium-low heat. Add onion, cover and cook until tender, about 10 minutes. Increase heat to medium-high, add ground meat and brown, stirring with fork. Add garlic and cinnamon and stir through. Season with salt and pepper to taste. Stir in 1 tablespoon tomato paste. Add rice, ½ cup tomato sauce and beef stock. Increase heat to high and bring mixture to boil. Reduce heat to low, cover and simmer until rice is partially cooked, about 5 to 7 minutes. Remove from heat and stir in pine nuts. Let cool slightly.

Grease roasting pan. Place 1 tablespoon meat mixture near one end of each cabbage leaf. Roll up, tucking in sides, to make small packets. Arrange in 2 layers in pan, packing tightly.

Preheat oven to 350°F. Combine 1 cup tomato sauce with remaining 1 tablespoon tomato paste in small bowl. Pour over cabbage, adding more tomato sauce as necessary to cover. Dot with butter. Cover pan, place over high heat and bring to boil. Transfer to oven and bake until tender, about 1 hour. Arrange lemon slices over top or pass Greek lemon sauce separately.

*Greek Lemon Sauce

---

3 **eggs**	1½ **cups hot chicken stock**
2½ **tablespoons fresh lemon juice**	

Beat eggs in large bowl until thick and lemon colored. Gradually beat in lemon juice. Add stock 1 tablespoon at a time, beating constantly. Transfer to small saucepan. Place over low heat and cook, stirring constantly, until sauce thickens. Serve immediately.

Broccoli Beef

4 servings

1 **pound fresh broccoli, trimmed and peeled**	¼ **cup diced pimiento**
	Chow Sauce*
1 **tablespoon vegetable oil**	**Chow mein noodles or freshly steamed rice**
2 **garlic cloves, minced**	
8 **ounces lean beef, thinly sliced**	
½ **cup frozen whole pearl onions, thawed and drained**	

Cook broccoli in boiling water until crisp-tender, about 10 minutes. Drain. Cut off florets; slice stems diagonally.

Heat wok or skillet over high heat. Add oil and swirl to coat. Add half of garlic and stir-fry briefly; do not burn. Blend in beef and broccoli stems and stir-fry about 2 minutes. Add florets, onions, pimiento and chow sauce. Cover and cook until vegetables are crisp-tender, 2 minutes. Serve over noodles or rice.

*Chow Sauce

---

2 **tablespoons oyster sauce**	1 **teaspoon cornstarch**
2 **tablespoons Chinese rice wine**	½ **teaspoon salt**
1 **tablespoon soy sauce**	

Mix all ingredients in small bowl.

Carbonnade Flamande

Beer is used to braise the meat for this classic Belgian beef stew. Whipped potatoes are traditionally piped directly onto the stew for a dramatic look.

8 servings

2 cups cold water
2 ounces salt pork or fatback, cut into ¼-inch cubes

3 tablespoons vegetable oil
2 garlic cloves, halved
4 pounds lean beef stew meat, cut into 1½-inch cubes
1 tablespoon all purpose flour
¼ teaspoon freshly ground pepper

2 12-ounce bottles dark beer
¼ cup red wine vinegar
3 tablespoons Dijon mustard
3 bay leaves

½ teaspoon dried thyme, crumbled
2 tablespoons (¼ stick) unsalted butter
4 large onions, sliced into ¼-inch-thick rings
8 medium carrots, cut into ½-inch cubes
Water or beef stock (optional)

Potatoes Mont-Dore*
(omit broiling step)
Melted unsalted butter
(about ½ cup)

Bring water to boil with salt pork in medium saucepan over medium-high heat. Reduce heat and simmer 5 minutes. Drain and rinse salt pork under cold water. Pat dry. Transfer salt pork to deep, heavy Dutch oven.

Heat oil in heavy large skillet over medium heat. Add garlic and cook until golden brown, stirring occasionally. Discard garlic. Pat beef dry. Add beef to skillet in batches and brown well on all sides. Remove from skillet using slotted spoon and add to salt pork. Return beef to skillet with salt pork. Sprinkle with flour and stir to blend. Season with pepper. Cook 3 minutes, stirring occasionally. Return mixture to Dutch oven using slotted spoon.

Degrease skillet. Place over medium-high heat, add beer and stir, scraping up any browned bits. Blend in vinegar, mustard, bay leaves and thyme. Pour beer over meat mixture. Melt butter in same skillet over medium-high heat. Add onions and sauté until golden brown, about 7 minutes. Mix onions into meat. Bring stew to simmer. Reduce heat to low, cover and cook until meat is tender, skimming fat as necessary, 1½ to 1¾ hours; add carrots during last 30 minutes of cooking time. If stew is too dry, add more water or beef stock as necessary. If too liquid, remove beef and vegetables using slotted spoon. Cook liquid uncovered until reduced to desired consistency. (*Stew can be prepared 2 to 3 days ahead and gently rewarmed over low heat.*)

Just before serving, preheat broiler. Transfer stew to broilerproof serving dish. Taste stew and adjust seasoning. Spoon hot potatoes into large pastry bag fitted with large star tip. Pipe potatoes around rim of stew. Drizzle potatoes with melted butter. Broil until lightly browned and serve. (Potatoes can be broiled separately; see recipe.)

*Potatoes Mont-Dore

Beaten egg whites give these mashed potatoes added lightness. Use as a topping for Carbonnade or as a side dish with chops and roasts.

8 servings

2 pounds potatoes, peeled and halved (or quartered depending on size)

2 eggs, separated, room temperature
¼ cup (½ stick) unsalted butter
Freshly grated nutmeg

Salt and freshly ground pepper
¾ to 1 cup milk, heated
⅛ teaspoon cream of tartar

½ cup (1 stick) unsalted butter, melted

Bring potatoes and salted water to cover to boil in large saucepan over medium-high heat. Reduce heat and simmer until tender, about 20 minutes.

Drain potatoes. Transfer to large bowl and beat with portable electric mixer at medium speed until smooth. Mix in yolks. Beat in ¼ cup butter with nutmeg, salt and pepper to taste. Gradually beat in ¾ cup milk (potatoes should be light but not loose; add remaining milk 1 tablespoon at a time as necessary). Beat whites with cream of tartar in another large bowl until stiff but not dry. Gently fold whites into potatoes.

Preheat broiler. Butter broilerproof gratin or other baking dish. Turn potato mixture into dish. Drizzle with melted butter. Broil until lightly browned and serve immediately.

Potatoes can be piped over Carbonnade Flamande and broiled (see recipe).

Caraway Beef Stew

6 to 8 servings

½ cup (1 stick) butter or margarine
3 pounds beef chuck, sirloin or top round, cut into 1-inch cubes
12 medium onions, sliced
2 tablespoons sweet paprika
1 tablespoon caraway seeds
1 tablespoon chopped fresh marjoram

2 teaspoons salt
Juice of ½ lemon
½ cup dry red wine
1 large garlic clove, crushed

1 tablespoon all purpose flour
1 tablespoon tomato paste
Chopped fresh parsley

Melt butter in Dutch oven until bubbly. Add meat all at once, turning until cooked on all sides. Mix in onions and half the paprika, caraway, marjoram, salt and lemon juice. Add wine and garlic. Simmer uncovered, stirring occasionally, until meat is tender, about 1½ to 2 hours.

Blend remaining paprika, caraway, marjoram, salt, flour and lemon juice with tomato paste and a bit of liquid from stew; add to meat. Simmer 15 minutes more. Sprinkle with parsley and serve.

Stew may be prepared the night before and reheated.

Hunter's One-Pot (Jäger Eintopf)

6 servings

3 tablespoons butter
3 tablespoons vegetable oil
1½ pounds beef bottom round (trimmed of all fat), cut into ¾-inch cubes and patted dry
2 medium onion, coarsely diced
3 tablespoons snipped fresh chives
4 tablespoons coarsely chopped fresh parsley
12 ounces mushrooms, trimmed and sliced
4 to 5 medium potatoes, peeled and diced

⅓ cup (or more) dry German white wine, preferably Riesling
1 teaspoon imported sweet paprika
¾ teaspoon salt
⅛ teaspoon freshly ground pepper
Generous pinch of freshly grated nutmeg
⅓ cup sour cream

Melt 1½ tablespoons butter with 1½ tablespoons oil in heavy large skillet over high heat. Add beef cubes in batches and brown on all sides. Transfer to 3- to 4-quart Dutch oven or flameproof casserole. Melt ½ tablespoon butter with ½ tablespoon oil in medium skillet over medium heat. Add onion, chives and 2 tablespoons parsley and cook 4 to 5 minutes. Add to meat. Melt remaining

1 tablespoon butter with 1 tablespoon oil in same skillet over medium heat. Add mushrooms and cook 4 to 5 minutes. Add to meat. Blend in potatoes.

Combine ⅓ cup wine with paprika, salt, pepper and nutmeg in small bowl. Pour over meat mixture and bring to boil over medium heat. Reduce heat to low, cover and simmer, stirring occasionally, 55 to 60 minutes, adding 1 or 2 tablespoons more wine if necessary. Remove from heat and stir in sour cream. Adjust seasoning. Transfer to soup tureen or serve from Dutch oven. Garnish with remaining chopped parsley and serve immediately.

Russian Cholent

A traditional Jewish Sabbath dish.

6 servings

2 tablespoons vegetable oil
3 pounds beef short ribs, cut into 2-inch pieces and patted dry with paper towels
3 large onions, chopped
1½ cups water
3 teaspoons Hungarian sweet paprika
1½ teaspoons salt
½ teaspoon freshly ground pepper

2 large potatoes, peeled and quartered lengthwise
⅓ cup pearl barley
1 10-ounce package frozen lima beans or 10 ounces cooked fresh lima beans

Heat oil in Dutch oven over medium heat. Add rib pieces and brown well, about 6 minutes on each side. Add chopped onion and sauté until browned, about 10 minutes. Add water, 2 teaspoons paprika, ½ teaspoon salt and ½ teaspoon freshly ground pepper. Cover and simmer 1½ hours.

Add potatoes, barley, remaining 1 teaspoon paprika and 1 teaspoon salt. Cover and continue simmering until ribs and potatoes are tender, about 30 minutes. Stir in lima beans. Cook until beans are tender, about 10 minutes. Skim accumulated fat from surface and discard. Serve cholent hot.

Braised Oxtails with Gremolata and Spinach Fettuccine

The tangy gremolata, a blend of parsley, garlic and lemon, is a favorite of Italian cooks. It is traditionally used as a topping for veal shanks, or osso buco.

6 to 8 servings

4 pounds oxtails, cut into 2-inch lengths
2 cups dry white wine
1½ cups dry red wine
4 large onions, coarsely chopped
4 large carrots, coarsely chopped
4 tablespoons (or more) olive oil
½ teaspoon dried rosemary, crumbled
½ teaspoon dried thyme, crumbled
4 garlic cloves, crushed
4 black peppercorns

4 cups beef or chicken stock
1 bouquet garni (1 parsley sprig, 1 thyme sprig, ½ bay leaf)

Salt and freshly ground pepper
2 tablespoons (¼ stick) unsalted butter, room temperature
2 tablespoons all purpose flour

Gremolata
¼ cup minced fresh parsley
4 garlic cloves, minced
1 teaspoon finely grated lemon peel

1 pound spinach fettuccine
2 tablespoons (¼ stick) butter or olive oil
Lemon slices and rosemary or thyme sprigs (garnish)

Combine oxtails, white and red wine, half of onions, half of carrots, 2 tablespoons olive oil, rosemary, thyme, garlic and peppercorns in large nonaluminum bowl. Cover and chill 3 hours, turning oxtails occasionally.

Drain oxtails, reserving 1½ cups marinade. Pat oxtails dry. Heat 2 tablespoons olive oil in Dutch oven over medium-high heat. Add oxtails in batches and brown on all sides, adding more oil to pan as necessary (place cooked oxtails in large bowl). Return to Dutch oven along with any juices in bottom of bowl. Add remaining carrots and onions, reserved marinade, beef stock and bouquet garni. Reduce heat, cover and simmer until oxtails are tender, 3 to 3½ hours.

Remove oxtails and vegetables from Dutch oven. Degrease cooking liquid. Boil until reduced to 2 cups. Season with salt and pepper. Remove from heat. Blend butter and flour to paste. Whisk into liquid a little at a time and blend until thickened. Return oxtails and vegetables to Dutch oven. Rewarm over low heat 10 minutes.

For gremolata: Mix parsley, garlic and peel. Stir into oxtails; heat 2 minutes.

Cook fettuccine in large amount of boiling salted water until just tender but firm to bite. Drain well. Toss immediately with butter or olive oil. Mound in center of platter. Top with oxtails. Garnish with lemon and rosemary and serve.

Baeckaoffa (Wine-braised Meat Stew)

Accompany this hearty one-dish meal with a mixed green salad.

4 to 6 servings

1 pound boneless beef chuck, cut into 2-inch pieces
8 ounces boneless pork shoulder, cut into 2-inch pieces
8 ounces boneless lamb shoulder, cut into 2-inch pieces
1 cup Sylvaner or other Alsatian dry white wine
2 tablespoons minced fresh parsley
½ bay leaf

¼ teaspoon dried thyme, crumbled
¼ teaspoon salt
¼ teaspoon freshly ground pepper

4 large onions, thinly sliced
4 large baking potatoes, peeled and thinly sliced

Combine meats, wine, parsley, bay leaf, thyme, salt and pepper in large bowl. Marinate in refrigerator overnight, stirring occasionally.

Preheat oven to 350°F. Butter 5-quart casserole. Cover bottom with ¼ of onions and ¼ of potatoes. Top with ⅓ of combined meats using slotted spoon. Continue with 3 more vegetable layers and 2 more meat layers. Pour in marinade. Cover casserole and bake until meat is tender, about 1½ hours. Serve stew directly from casserole.

Bollito Misto

A grand presentation for a special party. Cook uncovered so the broth reduces and develops a rich flavor.

8 servings

1 3- to 3½-pound beef tongue
1 beef or veal knuckle, halved
1 large onion, quartered
1 large carrot, quartered
2 celery stalks, cut into 2-inch pieces
2 tablespoons coarse salt

1 2-pound beef brisket, rolled and tied

1 cotechino sausage*
3 quarts water

1 3½-pound chicken
2 to 3 quarts chicken stock

1 large carrot, cut into ¼-inch-thick rounds
8 1- to 1½-inch-thick marrow bones
10 medium carrots with 2 inches of tops
10 small leeks, cut halfway through lengthwise, rinsed
10 small red potatoes

Salsa Verde and Salsa Rossa (see following recipes)

Combine tongue, beef knuckle, onion, 1 carrot, celery and salt in 16-quart stockpot. Add enough cold water to cover by 3 inches. Bring to boil, skimming surface. Reduce heat and simmer gently 1 hour.

Remove tongue; cut and peel off skin, fat and gristle while hot. Return tongue to pot and bring to simmer. Add brisket and enough boiling water to cover by 1 inch if necessary. Return to boil, skimming surface. Reduce heat and simmer gently, uncovered, 1¼ hours. (*Can be prepared 1 day ahead. Cool and refrigerate. Bring bollito to simmer before continuing.*)

Meanwhile, combine sausage and 3 quarts water in large saucepan and bring to boil. Reduce heat and simmer gently 2 hours; do not pierce sausage. Peel while hot. Return to cooking liquid. (*Cotechino sausage can be prepared 1 day ahead and refrigerated.*)

Add chicken to stockpot with tongue and brisket. Add enough boiling water to cover by 1 inch if necessary. Simmer until juices run clear when chicken is pierced in thickest part, about 45 minutes. Ladle off 2 to 3 quarts beef and chicken cooking liquid and reserve for another use. Discard vegetables. Add enough chicken stock to pot to cover chicken and meats by 1 inch if necessary. (*Can be prepared 4 hours ahead and refrigerated.*)

Place carrot round over both openings in marrow bones and tie in place with string. Tie medium carrots in bundles with string, leaving 1 long end. Tie leeks in bundles with string, leaving 1 long end. Cover potatoes with cold salted water in large saucepan. Boil until tender, about 20 minutes.

Meanwhile, bring brisket mixture to gentle simmer. Add carrots and leeks, tying long end of string to pot handle. Cook until vegetables are tender and meats are hot, about 15 minutes. Cook marrow bones in saucepan of boiling salted water 15 minutes. Simmer sausage until hot, about 10 minutes.

Remove strings from carrots and leeks. Cut chicken into serving pieces and sausage into ½-inch-thick slices. Arrange chicken, sausage, meats, vegetables and marrow bones on heated platter. Serve immediately, slicing tongue and brisket at table. Pass Salsa Verde and Salsa Rossa separately.

*Fresh Italian pork sausage. Available at some butcher shops and Italian markets.

Salsa Verde

Makes about ²/₃ cup

1 large garlic clove
1 2-ounce can anchovy fillets, drained
2 tablespoons capers, drained
1 teaspoon Italian wine vinegar or Sherry vinegar

½ teaspoon Dijon mustard
½ cup minced fresh parsley
⅓ cup (about) olive oil

Finely mince garlic in processor. Scrape down sides of work bowl. Add anchovies and capers and puree. Transfer mixture to small bowl. Whisk in vinegar and mustard. Add parsley, pressing mixture against sides of bowl to blend flavors. Vigorously stir in enough oil to make thin paste. Film top with oil. Cover tightly and refrigerate 8 hours or overnight.

Let sauce stand at room temperature 2 hours before using. Stir through several times just before serving.

Salsa Rossa

Also delicious with cold cuts or pasta.

Makes about 4 cups

¼ cup corn oil
1 large garlic clove, minced
2 medium onions, thinly sliced
1 celery stalk, finely diced
12 Italian plum tomatoes, peeled, seeded and coarsely chopped, or

two 28-ounce cans, drained, seeded and coarsely chopped
10 whole fresh basil leaves or ½ teaspoon dried, crumbled
1 tablespoon coarse salt

Heat oil in heavy medium saucepan over medium-low heat. Add garlic and sauté 1 minute. Add onions, cover and cook 5 minutes, stirring occasionally. Uncover and cook until tender, stirring frequently, about 10 minutes. Add celery and cook until tender, stirring frequently, about 10 minutes. Mix in tomatoes, basil and salt. Reduce heat, cover and simmer 30 minutes, stirring occasionally. Serve sauce warm or at room temperature.

Veal Breast Stuffed with Fresh Fennel Soufflé

Have your butcher crack the rib bones and make a pocket for the stuffing. This recipe can easily be halved.

6 to 8 servings

2 teaspoons crushed fennel seeds
1 teaspoon dried thyme, crumbled
½ teaspoon freshly ground pepper
1 7- to 7½-pound veal breast

Fresh Fennel Soufflé
3 tablespoons unsalted butter
1 large fennel bulb (tough outer ribs discarded), peeled, cored and coarsely chopped
1 medium onion, coarsely chopped
1 garlic clove, minced
2 tablespoons minced fresh parsley
¾ teaspoon finely crushed fennel seeds
¼ teaspoon dried thyme, crumbled
⅛ teaspoon freshly ground pepper
Pinch of ground mace

4 cups fresh breadcrumbs
⅓ cup whipping cream or half and half
3 eggs, separated, room temperature

¼ teaspoon salt
Pinch of cream of tartar

Butter
1 cup water
¼ cup dry vermouth

Vegetable Garnish
3 tablespoons unsalted butter
1 large fennel bulb (tough outer ribs discarded), peeled, quartered lengthwise, cored, then sliced crosswise ½ inch thick
2 medium-size red bell peppers, quartered lengthwise, then sliced crosswise ½ inch thick
2 medium-size green bell peppers, quartered lengthwise, then sliced crosswise ½ inch thick
1 teaspoon fennel seeds
1 teaspoon salt
⅛ teaspoon freshly ground pepper

Mix 2 teaspoons fennel seeds, 1 teaspoon thyme and ½ teaspoon pepper. Rub over inside and outside of veal. Let stand at room temperature while preparing fennel soufflé.

For soufflé: Melt 3 tablespoons butter in heavy large skillet over medium-low heat. Add fennel, onion and garlic and cook until golden brown, stirring frequently, about 10 minutes. Mix in parsley, fennel seeds, thyme, pepper and mace. Cover and cook until vegetables are very soft, stirring occasionally, about 20 minutes.

Puree fennel mixture in processor. Mix in breadcrumbs with 1 on/off turn. Blend in cream and yolks with several on/off turns. Transfer mixture to large bowl. (*Can be prepared 1 day ahead. Cool completely and refrigerate. Bring fennel mixture to room temperature before continuing with recipe.*)

Preheat oven to 450°F. In medium bowl of electric mixer, beat whites with salt and cream of tartar to soft peaks. Fold 1 cup whites into fennel mixture to loosen. Gently fold in remaining whites. Stand veal on closed end. Spoon fennel soufflé into pocket, shaking mixture down, filling to within 1 inch of top. Skewer pocket closed and lace tightly.

Set veal rib side down in large shallow roasting pan. Rub generously with butter. Roast 30 minutes. Reduce oven temperature to 350°F. Add water and vermouth to pan. Cover tightly with foil. Braise veal until very tender, about 2½ hours. Uncover veal and let stand for 20 minutes.

For garnish: Melt butter in heavy large skillet over medium-low heat. Add fennel and cook 5 minutes, stirring occasionally. Add peppers, fennel seeds, salt and pepper and cook until vegetables are crisp-tender, stirring occasionally, about 5 minutes.

Remove skewers and twine from veal. Set veal on platter. Surround with vegetable garnish. Strain pan juices. Pour into gravy boat and pass separately.

Braised Veal Shanks on Couscous

Harissa (page 112), the North African red pepper condiment, would be a zippy accompaniment to this hearty combination.

6 servings

6 **pounds veal shanks, cut into 2-inch lengths and tied around center**
½ **cup all purpose flour**
¼ **teaspoon salt**
⅛ **teaspoon freshly ground pepper**
2 **tablespoons (¼ stick) unsalted butter**
2 **tablespoons vegetable oil**
1 **cup dry white wine**
4 **cups beef stock**
3 **tablespoons tomato paste**
¼ **teaspoon saffron threads, crushed and dissolved in 1 tablespoon warm water**
¼ **teaspoon cinnamon**
8 **ounces butternut squash, peeled, seeded and coarsely chopped**
2 **large carrots, coarsely chopped**

2 **medium onions, coarsely chopped**
2 **small white turnips, peeled and coarsely chopped**
1 **medium zucchini, chopped**
10 **parsley sprigs, tied**
3 **large garlic cloves, halved**
2 **2-inch orange peel strips**

3 **cups couscous, cooked**
¼ **cup minced fresh cilantro or parsley**
8 **ounces baby carrots, boiled until tender**
8 **ounces baby white turnips, peeled, boiled until tender**
8 **ounces butternut squash, peeled, seeded, cut into 1-inch cubes and boiled until tender**

Pat veal dry. Combine flour, salt and pepper. Dredge veal in seasoned flour, patting off excess. Melt butter with oil in Dutch oven over medium-high heat. Add veal in batches and brown on all sides. Transfer to large bowl. Stir wine into Dutch oven and boil 1 minute. Return veal to Dutch oven along with any juices in bowl. Blend in stock, tomato paste, saffron and cinnamon. Add chopped vegetables, parsley, garlic and orange peel; bring to boil. Reduce heat, cover and simmer until veal and vegetables are very tender, 1½ to 2 hours.

Transfer veal to large bowl and cover with foil. Place vegetables in processor or blender. Degrease cooking liquid, then boil until reduced to 3½ cups. Discard parsley and orange peel. Add 1 cup liquid to vegetables and puree until smooth. Return puree and veal to Dutch oven and mix well. Rewarm over low heat.

Mound couscous on large platter. Top with veal. Ladle some of gravy over. Sprinkle with cilantro. Garnish with clusters of boiled carrots, turnips and butternut squash and serve. Pass remaining sauce separately.

Savory Veal One-Pot (Eingemachtes Kalbfleisch)

4 to 5 servings

1¾ pounds stewing veal (cut from shoulder or breast), trimmed and cut into 1¼-inch cubes
2 tablespoons (¼ stick) butter
1 small onion, finely chopped
¾ cup water
7 to 8 peppercorns, finely crushed
3 ¼-inch-thick strips lemon peel
1 small bay leaf
½ teaspoon salt
   Pinch of sugar

3 tablespoons butter
8 ounces small mushrooms, trimmed

3 leeks (with some of green), cut into ¾-inch lengths
1 cup fresh cauliflower florets

Sauce
1 tablespoon butter
1 tablespoon all purpose flour
1 egg yolk, lightly beaten
2 tablespoons whipping cream
1 tablespoon chopped capers
   Juice of ½ lemon
   Salt
1½ teaspoons chopped fresh parsley
   Lemon wedges

Combine veal in 3-quart Dutch oven or flameproof casserole with enough water to cover. Place over medium heat and bring to boil. Let boil 5 minutes. Drain veal well. Rinse out Dutch oven and return to medium heat. Add 2 tablespoons butter and stir until melted. Blend in onion and cook 3 to 4 minutes. Add water and veal. Stir in peppercorns, lemon peel, bay leaf, salt and sugar and bring to boil. Reduce heat to low, cover and simmer 1 hour.

Melt 3 tablespoons butter in medium skillet over medium-high heat. Add mushrooms and cook 3 to 4 minutes; set aside (do not wipe out skillet). Remove lemon peel and bay leaf from broth and discard. Layer mushrooms, leek and cauliflower in Dutch oven. Cover and cook until vegetables are tender, about 15 minutes.

For sauce: About 5 minutes before vegetables are done, melt 1 tablespoon butter in same skillet over medium heat. Stir in flour and mix until smooth. Cook about 2 minutes. Gradually drain broth from Dutch oven into flour mixture and stir until sauce is smooth. Combine egg yolk and cream in small bowl. Slowly stir ¼ cup sauce into egg mixture. Gradually add egg mixture to sauce, stirring constantly. Mix in capers and lemon juice. Remove from heat. Taste and season with salt. Transfer veal and vegetables to serving dish. Pour sauce over top. Sprinkle with chopped parsley, garnish with lemon wedges and serve immediately.

🍎 Pork, Sausage and Ham

Hot Garlic Eggplant

For variation, use shrimp instead of pork. Add to wok just before serving.

4 servings

5 to 6 ounces ground pork
2 teaspoons heavy soy sauce

1½ pounds eggplant (preferably oriental), trimmed
1 large yellow onion, cut into ½-inch cubes

¼ cup (or more) dry Sherry
3 tablespoons oyster sauce
1 tablespoon heavy soy sauce

2 teaspoons sesame oil
1 teaspoon sugar

3 tablespoons peanut oil
10 garlic cloves, finely minced
1 tablespoon chili paste with garlic
⅓ to ½ teaspoon minced fresh ginger

Chicken stock (optional)

Mix pork and 2 teaspoons soy sauce in small bowl and set aside.

Quarter each unpeeled oriental eggplant lengthwise. Place strips together and cut crosswise into ½-inch pieces. (If using large globe eggplant, peel and cut into ½-inch squares.) Transfer to medium bowl. Blend in onion.

Combine ¼ cup Sherry with oyster sauce, soy sauce, sesame oil and sugar in another small bowl. Set sauce aside.

Heat wok until very hot. Pour in peanut oil. Add garlic, chili paste and ginger and cook several seconds; do not allow garlic and ginger to brown.

Add pork mixture and stir-fry, pressing pork against sides of wok until meat loses raw color. Add eggplant mixture. Stir in sauce, adding more Sherry if necessary so liquid covers about half of stir-fry mixture.

Cover and cook over high heat until eggplant softens and is no longer raw tasting, about 3 minutes for oriental eggplant or 5 minutes for large globe type. If wok becomes dry during cooking, add small amount of Sherry or chicken stock. Continue cooking uncovered until most of sauce evaporates. Taste and adjust seasoning. Turn into dish and serve immediately.

Northern-style Chinese One-Pot

8 servings

¼ cup vegetable oil
1 pound ground pork
2 cups chopped cabbage
1 large onion, chopped
1 large carrot, shredded
5 to 6 ounces green beans, French-cut and sliced into 1-inch pieces
3 or 4 dried oriental black mushrooms, soaked in hot water 30 minutes, well drained and minced

1 teaspoon minced fresh ginger
¼ cup soy sauce
1½ cups uncooked rice
2 cups chicken stock
2 small zucchini, shredded
Salt and freshly ground pepper
Soy sauce (optional)
Minced green onion

Heat oil in wok or large skillet over medium-high heat. Add pork and stir until meat loses pink color. Stir in cabbage, onion, carrot, beans, mushrooms and ginger and stir-fry 2 minutes. Mix in soy sauce. Add rice and stir gently. Pour in stock. Cover tightly and simmer until liquid is almost absorbed, about 20 to 25 minutes. Stir in zucchini and cook about 5 minutes longer. Season with salt and pepper, and soy sauce if desired. Sprinkle with green onion and serve immediately.

Sauerkraut and Pork Gulyás with Sour Cream (Székelygulyás)

Serve with potatoes or noodles. Have the butcher cut the spareribs for you.

6 servings

¼ cup vegetable oil, bacon fat or lard
4 medium onions, coarsely chopped
6 garlic cloves, minced
⅛ teaspoon caraway seeds
2 tablespoons Hungarian sweet or medium-hot paprika
5 cups chicken stock
6 tablespoons chopped drained canned tomatoes or tomato puree
2 pounds lean pork shoulder, cut into 1-inch cubes

1½ pounds spareribs, halved crosswise and separated
1 pound unsmoked bacon, diced
3 pounds fresh sauerkraut,* rinsed under cold water, drained and squeezed dry
2 medium-size red bell peppers, slivered
3 cups sour cream
6 tablespoons all purpose flour
Salt and freshly ground pepper
Minced fresh parsley

Heat oil in heavy large pot over medium-low heat. Add onions and cook until translucent, stirring occasionally, about 10 minutes. Add garlic and caraway seeds and stir 1 minute. Stir in paprika. Add 2 cups stock and tomatoes and bring to boil. Stir in pork, ribs and bacon. Pour in more stock if necessary to keep meats partially covered. Reduce heat, cover and simmer until meats are almost tender, about 55 minutes.

Add sauerkraut and bell peppers to meat mixture. Pour in enough stock to just cover ingredients. Simmer until meats and sauerkraut are tender, skimming fat, about 30 minutes.

Blend 1½ cups sour cream and flour until smooth. Stir into gulyás. Simmer 5 minutes. Season with salt and pepper. Ladle into bowls. Top with dollops of remaining sour cream. Sprinkle with parsley and serve.

*Available in vacuum pouches at butcher shops and specialty foods stores.

Sweet and Sour Spareribs on Peppery Pickled Cabbage

6 servings

⅓ cup syrupy rice wine (*mirin*)*
⅓ cup cider vinegar
¼ cup dark soy sauce
2 tablespoons oriental sesame oil*
2 tablespoons firmly packed light brown sugar
1 1-inch cube peeled fresh ginger
1 small garlic clove
4 cups firmly packed fresh sauerkraut, rinsed, drained and squeezed dry
¼ teaspoon crushed red pepper flakes

6 pounds spareribs, cut into 2-rib widths

1½ cups firmly packed light brown sugar
1 cup dark soy sauce
½ cup fresh orange juice
¼ cup medium-dry Sherry
¼ cup rice vinegar
2 tablespoons tomato paste
2 tablespoons minced fresh ginger
8 large garlic cloves, halved

½ cup minced green onion

Blend first 7 ingredients in processor 30 seconds, scraping down sides of bowl. Pour into large nonaluminum bowl. Add sauerkraut and pepper flakes. Cover and refrigerate at least 3 hours, stirring occasionally. Let stand at room temperature at least 1 hour. (*Can be prepared 1 day ahead.*)

Preheat oven to 375°F. Arrange spareribs in single layer in large shallow roasting pan. Cover with cold water. Cover with foil and bake until ribs are tender, about 1½ hours. (*Can be prepared 1 day ahead and refrigerated.*) Pour off cooking liquid; degrease and reserve 1 cup. Reduce oven to 350°F.

Combine reserved cooking liquid, sugar, soy sauce, orange juice, Sherry, vinegar, tomato paste, ginger and garlic in heavy medium saucepan and stir over low heat until sugar dissolves. Pour over ribs. Bake uncovered for 1 hour, basting every 15 minutes.

Strain pan juices back into saucepan. Cover ribs with foil and keep warm. Boil juices over medium heat until reduced to 1½ cups, 10 to 15 minutes.

Mound sauerkraut on deep platter. Arrange ribs on top. Pour sauce over. Sprinkle with green onion and serve.

*Available at oriental markets.

Ragout of Pork Catalan

This Spanish-inspired stew gets its complex flavor from a wealth of seasonings and a day on both ends of the cooking—one to marinate and one to let the flavors develop. Pass saffron rice separately as an accompaniment.

12 servings

5 pounds boneless pork loin or shoulder, cut into 1½-inch cubes
1½ cups pitted prunes
1 cup Greek olives packed in brine, drained
1 7-ounce jar roasted red peppers, drained and chopped
⅓ cup red wine vinegar
⅓ cup olive oil
1 3½-ounce jar capers with 4½ teaspoons liquid
3 tablespoons minced garlic
3 tablespoons dried oregano, crumbled

1 tablespoon pure ground hot chili powder*

2 tomatoes, peeled and diced
1 cup dry white wine
½ cup firmly packed brown sugar
½ cup (or more) concentrated beef stock

2 tablespoons red wine vinegar
2 tablespoons water
2 tablespoons all purpose flour
Chopped fresh cilantro or parsley

Mix first 10 ingredients in large nonaluminum bowl. Cover and refrigerate overnight, turning occasionally.

Preheat oven to 325°F. Transfer pork mixture to 7- to 8-quart Dutch oven. Mix in tomatoes, wine, sugar and ½ cup stock. Bring to boil over high heat. Cover and bake 45 minutes, adding more stock if necessary to keep meat just covered. Uncover pan and cook until meat is tender, about 15 minutes. Cool to room temperature. Cover and refrigerate overnight.

Degrease stew. Bring to boil over medium heat. Gradually add 2 tablespoons vinegar and 2 tablespoons water to flour in small bowl to form paste. Gradually stir into stew. Reduce heat and simmer until sauce thickens slightly, stirring frequently, about 5 minutes. Top with cilantro and serve.

*Available at specialty foods stores and some supermarkets. Cayenne pepper can be substituted; add to taste.

Ratatouille with Sausage

This lusty casserole perfumed with the herbs of Provence becomes a complete main dish when sausages are added. Lots of crusty French or Italian bread, a leafy green salad and a jug of red wine, followed by fruit and cheese, complete a menu that could be expanded to serve a multitude.

12 servings

2 large eggplants, peeled and cut into strips
8 medium zucchini, cut into ½-inch slices
All purpose flour
Olive oil
5 large onions, sliced
6 garlic cloves, minced
6 large green bell peppers, seeded and diced
8 large tomatoes, peeled, seeded and cut into strips

1 cup finely chopped fresh parsley
2 teaspoons dried oregano, crumbled
2 teaspoons dried thyme, crumbled
2 teaspoons dried basil, crumbled
Salt and freshly ground pepper

12 sweet Italian sausages

Chopped fresh parsley

Dredge eggplant and zucchini in flour. Heat oil in heavy large skillet and sauté eggplant and zucchini in batches over medium-high heat about 5 minutes. Remove and drain on paper towels. Sauté onion, garlic and green pepper in same oil until soft, adding more oil if needed. Do not clean skillet.

Preheat oven to 350°F. Layer sautéed vegetables, tomatoes, 1 cup parsley and seasonings in 6-quart casserole. Stir gently to mix. Cover and bake 35 minutes.

Meanwhile, sauté sausages in same skillet until browned. Remove from pan, drain on paper towels and cool. Slice ¼ inch thick and return to skillet. Sauté slices 2 to 3 minutes on each side, adding oil if needed.

After vegetables have baked 35 minutes, add sausage, pushing most of the slices down into the mixture but arranging some over casserole top. Return to oven and bake uncovered for 20 minutes. Sprinkle with parsley and serve.

Flavor improves by making casserole 24 hours ahead and refrigerating. Bring to room temperature before reheating.

Ham, Corn and Cheese Mélange

A hearty one-dish that could be assembled in advance and then baked. Serve with green salad and dark bread.

6 to 8 servings

4 eggs
1½ cups milk
1½ cups shredded Gruyère, Fontina or Swiss cheese
¼ teaspoon salt
¼ teaspoon freshly ground pepper
Pinch of sugar
Dash of red pepper sauce

2 cups fresh or thawed frozen corn kernels
4 green onions, minced
1½ cups coarsely chopped country ham

Preheat oven to 350°F. Grease shallow 2-quart baking dish. Beat eggs, milk, cheese and seasoning in large bowl. Stir in corn and green onion. Pour half into baking dish. Sprinkle ham over top. Pour in remaining custard. Bake until knife inserted in center comes out clean, about 45 to 60 minutes. Serve immediately.

Spanish Pork with Saffron and Potatoes

A chicory salad tossed with oil and vinegar offers fine contrast to this one-dish dinner. The recipe doubles easily for large gatherings. Choose a hearty Spanish red Rioja Reserva wine.

5 to 6 servings

3 tablespoons olive oil
3 pounds Boston butt or boned country-style spareribs, cut into 1 × 2-inch pieces
2 medium onions, chopped
1 small red bell pepper, seeded and cut into 1/2-inch squares
3 3 × 1-inch strips orange peel (colored part only)
1 heaping tablespoon minced fresh fennel fronds
1 large garlic clove, minced
1 3-inch fresh thyme sprig or pinch of dried, crumbled
1 bay leaf
1/2 cup dry vermouth
2 cups meat or poultry stock, preferably homemade

3 tomatoes (preferably Italian plum tomatoes), peeled, seeded and chopped
Generous pinch of crushed saffron threads dissolved in 1 tablespoon warm water
1 pound new potatoes, peeled and cut into 1-inch chunks
1 1/2 teaspoons olive oil
4 ounces large green beans, cut into 1-inch lengths
1 4-ounce fennel bulb (tough outer ribs discarded), peeled, trimmed and cut into 1-inch chunks
1/3 cup pitted green olives, halved lengthwise
Salt and freshly ground pepper

Heat 3 tablespoons olive oil in heavy large skillet over medium-high heat. Pat pork dry and brown in batches (do not crowd). Transfer to heavy 5-quart saucepan. Discard all but 2 tablespoons fat in skillet. Add onion and bell pepper and cook over medium-low heat until onion is soft and starting to brown, about 10 minutes. Add orange peel, fennel fronds, garlic, thyme and bay leaf and stir until orange becomes aromatic, about 30 seconds. Pour in vermouth. Bring to boil, scraping up any browned bits. Cook until liquid is reduced to glaze. Add stock, tomatoes and dissolved saffron and boil until reduced by 1/3, about 7 minutes. Pour over pork and bring to simmer. Reduce heat, cover partially and simmer 45 minutes, turning pork occasionally. Stir in potatoes. Cover partially and simmer 15 minutes, turning pork and potatoes occasionally.

Meanwhile, heat 1 1/2 teaspoons olive oil in heavy medium skillet over medium-high heat. Add green beans and fennel and sauté until beginning to brown, about 3 minutes. Stir into pork mixture. Cover partially and simmer until pork is tender, about 25 minutes. Add olives, salt and pepper. Taste and adjust seasoning. Degrease sauce. Turn into dish and serve immediately. (*Can be prepared 2 days ahead. Cool, cover and refrigerate. Rewarm over medium-low heat.*)

Pork and Bitter Melon Stew (Pakbet)

The melon lends distinctive flavor to this Filipino specialty.

12 servings

2 tablespoons vegetable oil
3 tablespoons *bagoong* (shrimp paste)* or one 2-ounce can anchovies, drained and minced
4 medium garlic cloves, pounded to paste in mortar with pestle
2 medium tomatoes, chopped
1 medium onion, chopped
1 1/2 pounds 1/2-inch-thick pork loin chops, boned and cut into 2 × 2-inch pieces

1 small eggplant, halved lengthwise and cut crosswise into 1/2-inch slices
1 8-inch-long bitter melon,** halved lengthwise, seeded and cut crosswise into 1/4-inch slices
1 cup small okra, trimmed
12 ounces spinach, stemmed

Heat oil in wok or heavy large skillet over medium heat. Add shrimp paste and garlic and stir 5 minutes. Mix in tomatoes and onion and stir-fry until tender, about 8 minutes. Add pork and cook until no longer pink, about 15 minutes, stirring frequently. Mix in eggplant and bitter melon. Cover and simmer until melon turns bright green, about 5 minutes. Add okra. Cover and simmer until vegetables are crisp-tender, about 5 minutes.

Arrange spinach atop mixture. Cover and cook until spinach wilts, about 2 minutes. Transfer pork to center of heated platter. Surround with cooked melon and vegetables and serve.

*Available at oriental markets and specialty produce stores.
**Yellowish-green fruit available at oriental markets and specialty stores.

Petit Cassoulet

2 to 3 servings

2 cups chicken stock
2 cups water
1 cup dried Great Northern beans

1 Cornish game hen

2 ounces salt pork,
   blanched and diced
1 large sweet Italian sausage

½ small onion, chopped
2 ounces ham, diced
1 large garlic clove, minced
¼ teaspoon dried thyme, crumbled
1 bouquet garni (white part of
   1 leek, 2 celery tops, 2 parsley
   sprigs, ½ bay leaf)

4 ounces boneless pork (from rib
   chop), cubed
4 ounces lamb stew meat, cubed
½ cup dry white wine

1 medium tomato, peeled,
   seeded and chopped
   Salt and freshly ground pepper
½ cup dry breadcrumbs
2 tablespoons minced fresh parsley

Bring stock and water to boil in heavy large saucepan. Stir in beans. Return to boil and cook 2 minutes. Remove from heat. Cover and let stand at room temperature 1 hour.

Preheat oven to 450°F. Set game hen on rack in small roasting pan in oven. Reduce temperature to 350°F. Roast hen until juices run clear when thigh is pierced, about 45 minutes. Let cool. Cut hen into 4 pieces; set aside.

Sauté salt pork in heavy medium skillet over medium heat until golden brown, about 8 minutes. Remove with slotted spoon and drain on paper towels. Pierce sausage. Add to same skillet and cook over medium heat until brown, turning frequently, about 8 minutes. Remove with slotted spoon and drain. Add salt pork and sausage to beans. Do not wash skillet.

Bring beans to boil, skimming surface as necessary. Reduce heat; add onion, ham, garlic, thyme and bouquet garni and simmer until beans are almost tender, about 40 minutes. Discard bouquet garni. Remove sausage, slice ½ inch thick and set aside. Drain beans, reserving liquid.

Brown pork in reserved skillet over medium-high heat. Remove with slotted spoon and drain on paper towels. Repeat with lamb. Pour off drippings and reserve. Deglaze skillet with 2 tablespoons wine, scraping up browned bits clinging to bottom. Set aside.

Preheat oven to 350°F. Spread ⅓ of beans in bottom of 2-quart flameproof baking dish. Layer with half of sausage slices, 2 pieces hen, half of pork and lamb and half of tomato. Season with salt and pepper. Repeat layering. Cover with final ⅓ of beans. Combine reserved bean liquid, deglazing liquid and remaining white wine and add just enough to cover ingredients. Sprinkle with half of breadcrumbs and parsley. Bring to boil over medium heat. Transfer to oven and bake 1 hour. Push breadcrumb crust down with back of spoon. Sprinkle with remaining breadcrumbs and parsley. Drizzle with some of reserved drippings. Bake until second crust forms, about 30 minutes. Serve hot.

Garlic Pork with Rice and Black Beans (Puerco con Arroz y Frijol)

Interesting flavors and textures mingle in this one-pot dish: Spoon the pork and beans into warmed tortillas; serve the rich broth in which they were cooked as a soup alongside. Rice and salpicón are tasty "extras."

8 to 10 servings

8 quarts cold water
1 pound 6 ounces black beans, rinsed and sorted

1 large onion, roasted and unpeeled (see Tips and Techniques, page 107)
2 garlic heads, roasted and unpeeled
4 epazote sprigs* (optional)

1 5-pound pork butt, boned, trimmed and cut into 1½-inch cubes, bones reserved
Salt

Black Rice
⅓ cup vegetable oil
2 cups long-grain brown rice
2 garlic cloves, roasted, peeled and chopped
1 teaspoon salt

Salpicón (see following recipe)
24 corn or flour tortillas, warmed

Boil water with beans in 12-quart pot 10 minutes. Let steep 1 hour.

Add onion, garlic and epazote to beans. Bring to boil, reduce heat, cover partially and simmer 2 hours.

Add pork and bones and continue cooking until beans are tender and pork is cooked through, about 1 hour. Season with salt. Measure 5 cups broth for rice. Discard bones. (*Can be prepared 1 day ahead. Cover and refrigerate.*)

For rice: Preheat oven to 350°F. Heat oil in heavy medium ovenproof saucepan over medium heat. Add rice, garlic and salt and stir until rice becomes translucent, about 4 minutes. Add reserved 5 cups broth and bring to boil. Cover and bake until rice absorbs all liquid, approximately 1¼ hours.

Reheat pork and bean mixture over medium heat, stirring occasionally. Discard onion and garlic if desired. Transfer pork and beans to opposite ends of large platter using slotted spoon. Spoon rice into center. Ladle broth into individual bowls. Serve immediately, passing Salpicón and tortillas separately.

*Epazote is a wild herb. Available in many Latin American markets.

Salpicón

8 servings

7 medium tomatoes, roasted and unpeeled
2 jalapeño or 4 serrano peppers, roasted, peeled and chopped
2 large red onions, diced

2 avocados, peeled, pitted and sliced
4 limes, cut into wedges
12 ounces radishes, thinly sliced
1 cup cilantro, chopped

Mash 4 tomatoes in mortar with pestle or with back of spoon. Peel remaining 3 tomatoes and cut into wedges. Arrange all ingredients in separate bowls or in separate mounds on large platter.

🍎 *Tips and Techniques: Roasting Vegetables*

The recipes for Garlic Pork with Rice and Black Beans and Salpicón are adapted from ancient Mayan cookery. There are two easy methods to give onions, garlic, tomatoes and other vegetables the smoky flavor that underlies most Mayan recipes.

Gas stove method: Use long-handled fork or tongs to hold unpeeled vegetables over high flame and turn until charred, about 5 minutes for onions, 2½ minutes for tomatoes and 1½ minutes for garlic heads and chilies.

Electric stove method: Heat heavy large skillet over medium-high heat. Peel onions. Separate garlic heads into cloves and peel. Place onions, chilies and garlic in skillet and cook, turning frequently, until charred, 5 to 6 minutes for onions, about 3 minutes for chilies and about 1 minute for garlic cloves. Roast tomatoes separately, turning with spatula until well charred, about 8 minutes. Drain liquid from tomatoes.

Yugoslav Pork with String Beans

4 servings

Vegetable oil
1 large onion, thinly sliced
1 large green bell pepper (or 2 small), seeded and thinly sliced
1 pound pork tenderloin, cut into bite-size chunks
¼ to ½ teaspoon paprika
Salt and freshly ground pepper

8 ounces green beans, trimmed
½ cup water

2 tablespoons all purpose flour
Vegetable oil
Paprika
Sour cream

Heat small amount of oil in large skillet over medium-high heat. Add onion and green pepper and sauté until browned. Stir in pork, paprika, salt and pepper and continue cooking until meat is browned. Stir in beans and water, reduce heat, cover and simmer 45 minutes, or until pork is tender.

About 5 minutes before serving, brown flour in small amount of oil over low heat. Add paprika for color and stir constantly 2 to 3 minutes. Add to meat and continue cooking until sauce thickens. Serve hot topped with sour cream.

Skillet Sausage and Peppers

4 to 6 servings

2 tablespoons olive oil
1½ pounds hot or sweet Italian sausage
1 large green bell pepper, seeded and chopped
1 28-ounce can whole Italian tomatoes

1 medium-size yellow onion, chopped
½ cup dry red wine
Freshly cooked noodles

Heat olive oil in large skillet over medium-high heat. Add sausage and brown about 15 minutes. Drain excess oil. Add green pepper, tomatoes, onion and wine. Simmer over low heat, stirring occasionally, 30 minutes. Serve over noodles.

Vosges Mountain Sausage and Vegetable Pot

A hearty dinner that is best with beer, ale or a dry white wine.

5 to 6 servings

2 ⅛-inch-thick slices bacon, coarsely chopped
2 cups diced onion
¼ cup diced peeled celery root
1½ to 2 pounds smoked beef sausage, cut into ¾-inch-thick slices
3 cups water
¼ cup chopped fresh parsley
½ teaspoon black peppercorns, crushed
¼ teaspoon salt

4 to 5 medium carrots, coarsely sliced

2 medium parsnips, peeled and coarsely sliced
1 large rutabaga, peeled and very coarsely cubed
4 to 5 medium boiling potatoes, peeled and cut into eighths
1 small cabbage (about 1¼ pounds), cored and cut into 5 to 6 wedges
   Salt and freshly ground pepper
2 tablespoons minced fresh parsley

Brown bacon in 4-quart saucepan or Dutch oven over medium heat. Add onion and celery root and cook 2 minutes, stirring constantly. Stir in sausage, water, parsley, peppercorns and salt. Reduce heat, cover and simmer 20 minutes.

Add carrots, parsnips, rutabaga and potatoes. Cover and simmer 12 minutes. Arrange cabbage wedges over top, cover and continue cooking until cabbage is tender, about 15 minutes. Lightly season cabbage with salt and pepper. Sprinkle top with minced fresh parsley. Serve immediately.
Can be prepared ahead and reheated.

Swiss-style Scalloped Onions and Ham

A simple brunch or supper dish.

4 to 6 servings

6 tablespoons (¾ stick) unsalted butter
2½ pounds onions, thinly sliced
1 teaspoon sugar
   Salt

1 cup fresh white breadcrumbs, air-dried 2 hours

12 ounces smoked ham, cut into ¼-inch-thick shavings, some fat included

6 ounces Gruyère or Emmenthal cheese, grated
   Freshly ground pepper
   Freshly grated nutmeg
2 cups whipping cream, scalded

Melt 4 tablespoons butter in heavy large skillet over medium heat. Add onions and cook until softened, stirring frequently, about 10 minutes. Add sugar and cook until onions are light golden brown, stirring frequently, about 5 minutes. Season with salt.

Melt remaining 2 tablespoons butter in heavy small skillet over medium-high heat. Add breadcrumbs and stir until golden brown, about 5 minutes.

Preheat oven to 375°F. Using slotted spoon, transfer half of onions to large oval gratin dish or ovenproof baking dish. Top with half of ham and half of cheese. Season with salt, pepper and nutmeg. Repeat layering with remaining onions, ham and cheese. Cover with cream. Sprinkle with breadcrumbs. Bake until bubbling, lightly browned and cream is absorbed, about 35 minutes (time will vary somewhat depending on water content of onions). Let stand 15 minutes before serving.

❦ *Lamb and Rabbit*

Curry of Vegetables with Lamb

As with most curries, this one improves in flavor if prepared one day in advance (take care not to overcook the lamb, though). Serve with rice, beer and a salad of yogurt and cucumber spiked with some minced fresh mint.

8 servings

2 medium onions, coarsely chopped
1 tablespoon coarsely chopped fresh ginger
4 medium garlic cloves
2 dried hot red chilies, seeded and crushed (about 1½ teaspoons)
5 tablespoons vegetable oil
½ teaspoon freshly ground cardamom
Pinch of ground cloves
1½ pounds lamb (from shoulder, neck or shank), cut into small pieces*
2 cups meat or poultry stock
¾ cup coconut milk (preferably unsweetened)
½ cup lentils

2 tablespoons (¼ stick) butter
2 medium onions, sliced into thin rings (about 2 cups)
2 cups cauliflower florets (about 8 ounces)
2 cups coarsely chopped carrot or rutabaga (about 1 pound)

½ teaspoon *each* minced fresh ginger, black peppercorns and mustard seeds
⅛ teaspoon *each* whole allspice, caraway seeds, cumin seeds, cinnamon and turmeric
8 fennel seeds
½ cup meat or poultry stock

Puree chopped onion, chopped ginger, garlic and chilies in processor. Heat vegetable oil in large saucepan or Dutch oven over medium-high heat. Add puree, cover, reduce heat to medium-low and cook 20 minutes, stirring occasionally. Uncover and cook, stirring constantly, until moisture is evaporated, oil is beginning to separate and puree is beginning to fry, about 5 minutes (watch carefully so mixture does not burn). Sprinkle with cardamom and cloves and cook 30 seconds. Reduce heat to medium, add lamb and stir until meat just loses red color. Add 2 cups stock and coconut milk and bring to gentle simmer. Cover and cook until meat is barely tender, about 30 minutes. Add lentils, cover and continue cooking 30 minutes.

Melt butter in heavy nonaluminum large skillet over low heat. Add sliced onion, cover and cook until onion is soft and just beginning to color, about 10 minutes. Push onion to side of skillet and add cauliflower and carrot. Increase heat to medium and cook until vegetables are browned.

Meanwhile, combine minced ginger, peppercorns, mustard seeds, allspice, caraway, cumin, cinnamon, turmeric and fennel seeds in mortar or spice grinder and grind to powder. When cauliflower begins to brown, sprinkle spice mixture over vegetables and cook 4 to 5 minutes, stirring frequently (watch carefully so spices do not burn). Add ½ cup stock and stir, scraping up any browned bits. Bring mixture to boil. Pour over meat. Simmer over medium heat, uncovered, until vegetables are tender, about 20 minutes. Transfer curry to dish and serve.

*Although untraditional, an equal amount of beef or pork can be substituted.

Bosnian Hot Pot

6 to 8 servings

½ cup (1 stick) butter
1 large onion, sliced into
⅛-inch rings
2 large garlic cloves, minced
2 medium zucchini, sliced
¼ inch thick
2 tablespoons medium-hot
Hungarian paprika
Salt and freshly ground pepper
2 pounds boneless lamb, trimmed
and cut into 2-inch cubes

3 large ripe tomatoes, sliced
½ inch thick
1 medium-size red bell pepper,
seeded and sliced into
¼-inch rings
4 ounces cabbage,
coarsely shredded

1 teaspoon minced fresh parsley
½ teaspoon dried marjoram,
crumbled
½ teaspoon dried rosemary,
crumbled
4 ounces green beans, trimmed and
cut into thirds
2 medium-size green bell peppers,
seeded and sliced into
¼-inch rings
1 medium eggplant, peeled and
sliced ¼ inch thick
¾ cup rice
½ cup dry white wine
1 cup sour cream

Melt ¼ cup butter in heavy large skillet over medium heat. Add onion and garlic and stir until golden brown, about 5 minutes. Remove from skillet. Add zucchini and cook until lightly browned, stirring occasionally, about 5 minutes. Remove and set aside. Melt remaining ¼ cup butter in same skillet. Stir in paprika, salt and pepper and cook 1 minute. Add lamb and brown quickly on all sides. Remove and set aside.

Preheat oven to 350°F. Grease bottom and sides of large deep baking dish. Spread onion mixture over bottom. Layer with half of tomatoes, all of zucchini, red pepper and cabbage, seasoning each layer lightly with salt and pepper. Sprinkle cabbage with half of parsley, marjoram and rosemary. Continue layering with green beans, green peppers, eggplant and remaining tomatoes, seasoning each layer lightly with salt and pepper. Sprinkle tomatoes with remaining herbs. Top with rice, lamb and wine. Cover and bake until rice and meat are tender, basting frequently with liquid in dish, about 40 minutes. Serve immediately, passing sour cream separately.

Lamb Stew in the Moroccan Style

A selection of spicy North African salads would be a fitting prelude to this entrée. Serve the main course with steamed couscous or rice and a crisp red Rioja wine, and end with fresh fruit.

6 to 8 servings

3 pounds lamb (from shoulder,
neck, shank or leg), cut into
1-inch cubes
All purpose flour
7 tablespoons clarified butter

¼ teaspoon whole cumin seeds
1 1-inch piece cinnamon stick,
broken into pieces
3 whole coriander seeds
2 cardamom pods, shelled
6 whole peppercorns
2 medium to large onions, sliced

1 medium-size green bell
pepper, seeded and chopped
2 small garlic cloves, minced

2½ to 3 cups unsalted beef stock
reduced to 1½ cups
1½ to 2 tablespoons tomato paste

¼ teaspoon cayenne pepper
¼ cup firmly packed golden raisins
¼ cup toasted slivered almonds
Steamed couscous or rice

Coat lamb cubes with flour, shaking off excess. Melt 4 tablespoons butter in heavy large skillet over medium-high heat. Add lamb in batches and brown well on all sides (do not allow pieces to touch or they will steam rather than brown). Remove and set aside.

Finely pulverize cumin, cinnamon, coriander, cardamom and peppercorns in electric coffee grinder or with mortar and pestle. Heat 3 tablespoons butter in 4- to 5-quart heavy casserole over medium-low heat. Stir in onion and green pepper, cover and cook until vegetables are very limp. Stir in minced garlic, cover and cook for 3 minutes.

Add spice mixture to casserole and stir until well blended. Cover and cook until spices give off a pleasant aroma, about 1 to 2 minutes. Add lamb, stock and tomato paste and stir until well combined. Cover partially and simmer gently about 30 minutes.

Stir in cayenne. Cover partially and continue simmering until meat is tender, about 1 hour. Add raisins and almonds and cook 5 minutes longer. Serve hot, accompanied by mounds of steamed couscous or rice.

Stew can be prepared several days ahead and refrigerated.

Braised Lamb in Red Wine Sauce

Although this robust Portuguese stew is usually made with kid, the version here uses lamb shoulder, which is more readily available.

8 servings

4 pounds boned lean lamb shoulder, cut into 1½-inch cubes and patted dry
2 teaspoons salt
½ teaspoon freshly ground pepper
1 cup all purpose flour
6 tablespoons olive oil
2 tablespoons corn or vegetable oil
4 medium onions, coarsely chopped
2 medium carrots, coarsely chopped
1 medium-size red bell pepper, coarsely chopped
3 large garlic cloves, minced

2 tablespoons paprika
½ teaspoon cayenne pepper
1½ teaspoons dried marjoram, crumbled
½ teaspoon ground cumin
2 large bay leaves
3 cups beef stock
2 cups dry red wine
1 4-ounce piece of prosciutto, trimmed and cut into ½-inch cubes
Freshly cooked rice

Sprinkle lamb with salt and pepper. Dredge in flour, shaking off excess. Heat 4 tablespoons olive oil and 1 tablespoon corn oil in Dutch oven over medium heat. Add ⅓ of lamb and brown well on all sides. Transfer to bowl. Add 1 tablespoon olive oil and 1 tablespoon corn oil to Dutch oven. Add ⅓ of lamb and brown well on all sides. Transfer to bowl. Add remaining olive oil and lamb to Dutch oven and brown well on all sides. Transfer to bowl. Reduce heat to medium-low. Add onions, carrots, bell pepper and garlic to Dutch oven and cook until onions are soft and lightly browned, stirring occasionally, about 15 minutes.

Return lamb to Dutch oven along with juices in bowl. Stir in paprika and cayenne. Add marjoram, cumin and bay leaves and cook 3 minutes to blend flavors. Add stock, wine and prosciutto and bring to simmer. Cover and cook until lamb is very tender, adjusting heat so liquid bubbles gently, 2 to 2½ hours. Adjust seasoning. Serve with freshly cooked rice.

Braised Lamb and Batter-dipped Cauliflower

A Tunisian specialty.

6 servings

2 tablespoons olive oil
2 pounds boneless lamb (from leg), cut into 2-inch cubes
¼ cup chopped onion
2 garlic cloves, minced
¼ cup tomato paste
2 teaspoons Harissa (see following recipe), or ½ teaspoon freshly ground pepper
  Salt
2 cups water

2 pounds cauliflower, divided into florets

½ cup vegetable oil
½ cup milk
2 eggs, beaten to blend
3 tablespoons all purpose flour
¼ cup cooked garbanzo beans (chickpeas)
  Additional Harissa

Heat olive oil in heavy large skillet over medium heat. Add lamb, onion and garlic and cook 5 minutes, stirring frequently. Add tomato paste and harissa and cook 5 minutes, stirring frequently. Season generously with salt. Add water, cover and cook until lamb is tender, about 45 minutes.

Cook cauliflower in large amount of boiling water until crisp-tender. Drain.

Heat vegetable oil in heavy large skillet. Blend milk, eggs and flour until smooth. Dip cauliflower into batter. Add to oil in batches and brown well, about 2 minutes. Add cauliflower to lamb mixture using slotted spoon. Add garbanzos. Shake to mix; do not stir. Serve immediately, passing additional harissa separately.

Harissa

The classic—and fiery— North African condiment. The recipe doubles easily.

Makes about ⅔ cup

8 to 10 dried hot red chilies, preferably guajillo

1 tablespoon olive oil
4 garlic cloves

1 teaspoon ground coriander
1 teaspoon ground caraway seeds
½ teaspoon salt
2 tablespoons water

Stem and seed chilies. Break into pieces. Rinse under cold water. Let chilies stand 5 minutes; do not pat dry.

Combine chilies, oil, garlic, coriander, caraway and salt in processor and mix to paste; some texture should remain. Blend in water.

Harissa can be prepared 1 week ahead, covered and refrigerated.

Lemon Lamb with Potatoes

A Middle East-inspired lamb stew layered with potato slices. It can be partially prepared ahead and frozen, then assembled one to two days ahead. For a complete meal, add a green salad, a light red wine, pita bread and, for dessert, pineapple sprinkled with kirsch.

6 servings

¼ cup fresh lemon juice
1 tablespoon vegetable oil
1 large garlic clove, crushed
¼ teaspoon coriander seeds, ground
  Pinch of freshly ground pepper
2 pounds lamb (from neck, shoulder or shank), trimmed of excess fat and cut into 1-inch cubes

1 tablespoon butter
1 tablespoon vegetable oil
3 medium onions, chopped (about 3 cups)

⅛ teaspoon cumin seeds
  Pinch of ground allspice
2 cups beef stock
3 tablespoons tomato paste
  Salt

1½ pounds potatoes, boiled until tender, peeled and thinly sliced
4 scant tablespoons cilantro leaves
2 tablespoons fresh lemon juice

Combine ¼ cup lemon juice, 1 tablespoon oil, garlic, coriander and pepper in shallow large dish. Add lamb and stir to coat. Cover and refrigerate 24 hours, stirring mixture occasionally.

Remove meat from marinade using slotted spoon; reserve marinade. Pat meat dry. Heat butter and oil in heavy large skillet over medium-high heat. Add lamb in batches (do not crowd) and brown on all sides. Transfer to 3- to 4-quart saucepan or Dutch oven. Pour off all but thin film of fat from skillet. Place skillet over medium-low heat, add onion and cook until soft, stirring frequently. Blend in cumin and allspice and cook 30 seconds. Add stock, tomato paste and reserved marinade and stir, scraping up any browned bits. Bring mixture to boil. Pour over lamb. Season lightly with salt. Cover and simmer gently until lamb is tender, about 1½ hours. (*Can be prepared ahead and refrigerated several days.*)

To assemble: Grease 1½-quart soufflé dish or other deep baking dish. Arrange layer of potatoes in bottom of dish, overlapping slightly. Sprinkle lightly with salt. Top with half of lamb mixture using slotted spoon. Sprinkle with about 1 tablespoon cilantro. Sprinkle 1 tablespoon lemon juice over top. Repeat layering, ending with potato and reserving some cilantro for garnish. Spread sauce over top. (*Can be prepared 1 to 2 days ahead to this point and refrigerated. Bring to room temperature before continuing with recipe.*)

Preheat oven to 350°F. Cover baking dish with foil. Bake 45 minutes. Remove foil and continue baking 10 minutes. Sprinkle with remaining cilantro and serve.

Stifado

A robust Greek rabbit stew.

6 to 8 servings

2 rabbits (5 to 6 pounds total), cleaned and each cut into 8 to 9 pieces
2 cups red wine vinegar

½ cup vegetable oil
Salt and freshly ground pepper
All purpose flour

2½ tablespoons all purpose flour
1 cup dry white wine
½ cup Mavrodaphne wine*

5 tablespoons sugar
10 garlic cloves, minced
¼ cup tomato paste
5 to 6 bay leaves

½ cup vegetable oil
2½ pounds pearl onions, peeled

Cooked green beans or broccoli

Combine rabbit pieces and vinegar in large bowl. Cover and marinate in refrigerator 4 hours or overnight, turning occasionally.

Drain rabbit, discarding vinegar. Heat ½ cup oil in large skillet over high heat. Sprinkle rabbit with salt and pepper. Dredge lightly in flour, shaking off excess. Add to hot oil in batches and brown about 3 minutes on each side. Set rabbit aside. Remove skillet from heat. Strain oil and return to skillet. Add 2½ tablespoons flour and blend until smooth. Stir in wines, sugar, garlic, tomato paste, bay leaves and salt and freshly ground pepper to taste.

Heat remaining ½ cup oil in Dutch oven over medium-high heat. Add pearl onions and sauté until lightly browned on all sides. Discard excess oil. Add rabbit, wine mixture and enough water just to cover rabbit. Reduce heat to low, cover and simmer until rabbit is cooked through, about 45 minutes.

To serve, arrange rabbit pieces in center of heated platter. Pour sauce over. Surround with onions. Garnish with beans or broccoli.

*Dry Marsala can be substituted.

Lapin aux Pruneaux et au Céleri-Rave
(Stewed Rabbit with Prunes and Celery Root)

4 servings

18 pitted prunes
1 cup hard cider
(preferably imported)

2¼ pounds celery root, peeled and
cut into olive-shaped pieces
8 ounces pearl onions, peeled
8 tablespoons (1 stick) butter

1 2½- to 3-pound rabbit, cut into
8 serving pieces
Salt and freshly ground pepper
2 tablespoons cider vinegar

2 tablespoons applejack
3 cups veal stock
6 large shallots, minced
2 medium garlic cloves, crushed
Bouquet garni (12 parsley sprigs,
1 bay leaf and ½ teaspoon dried
thyme, crumbled)

12 slices white bread, cut with fluted
cutter into 2½- to 3-inch rounds

Minced fresh parsley

Soak prunes in ½ cup cider at least 2 hours, stirring occasionally.

Meanwhile, blanch celery root in boiling water until crisp-tender, about 15 minutes. Set aside. Cut cross in root ends of onions. Heat 2 tablespoons butter in heavy large skillet over medium-high heat. Add onions and sauté until golden, about 3 minutes. Remove onions using slotted spoon.

Heat same skillet over medium-high heat. Pat rabbit dry; add to skillet in batches (do not crowd) and brown on all sides, adding more butter if necessary. Return all rabbit pieces to pan. Season with salt and generous amount of pepper. Add remaining ½ cup hard cider, vinegar and applejack and boil until liquid is reduced to about 1 tablespoon. Add veal stock, shallots, garlic and bouquet garni and bring to boil. Reduce heat, cover and simmer mixture gently for 30 minutes.

Meanwhile, melt remaining butter in heavy large skillet over medium-high heat. Add bread rounds in batches and brown, about 1 minute per side.

Transfer rabbit to clean skillet. Strain liquid through fine sieve over rabbit. Add onions and celery root. Drain prunes, add to rabbit and bring mixture to boil. Reduce heat, cover and simmer until skewer inserted in thickest part of rabbit leg comes out easily, about 15 minutes. Transfer rabbit and vegetables to serving dish. Boil sauce until reduced to 2 cups. Pour over rabbit. Sprinkle with parsley, garnish with bread rounds and serve.

🍎 Index

❧ Credits and Acknowledgments

The following people contributed the recipes included in this book:

Terrie Achacoso
Ambassade d'Auvergne, Paris, France
Jean Anderson
A Shot of Class, Sacramento, California
Athenian Inn, Seattle, Washington
Nancy Baggett
Nancy Verde Barr
Louise Blackwell
Johanne Blais
Betsy Blankett
Emily Bradley
Connie de Brenes
Robert Broder
Patricia Brooks
James W. Burn
George Caloyannidis
Campbell's Place, Philadelphia,
    Pennsylvania
Hugh Carpenter
John Carter
Ginger Chang
Chiberta, Paris, France
Coconnas, Paris, France
Dinah Corley
Emilia Cortes
Maggi Dahlgren
Deirdre Davis
Four Seasons Olympic Hotel, Seattle,
    Washington
Nancy Friedlander
The Garden Room Cafe, Lakeport,
    California
Fred Gebhart
Cora Gemil
Judith Gerstein
Peggy Glass

Phyllis Gorenstein
Grandma's Saloon & Deli, Duluth,
    Minnesota
Freddi Greenberg
Anne Greer
Michel Guérard
Malcolm Hamilton
Cherry Hamman
Jim Hardeman
John Hartman
Jim Holmes
Christopher Horan
Janet Hurst
John Clancy's Restaurant, New York,
    New York
Madeleine Kamman
Barbara Karoff
Lynne Kasper
George Lang
Faye Levy
Leon Lianides
Mimmetta Lo Monte
Robert Magretta
Abby Mandel
Linda Marino
Copeland Marks
Naomi Marshall
Michael McCarty
Richard McCullough
Marty McDaniel
Janet McMillan
Shirley Metropoulos
Perla Meyers
Mark Miller
Toni Milto
Jefferson Morgan

Jinx Morgan
Doris Muscatine
Dolores Nash
Ruta Nonacs
Beatrice Ojakangas
Pat Opler
Marsha Palanci
Suzanne Paulson
Fenella Pearson
The Post House, Evergreen, Colorado
Ruedell Reaves
Phyllis Rizzi
Michael Roberts
Betty Rosbottom
Richard Sax
Edena Sheldon
Lari Siler
Susan Slack
Shirley Slater
Andre Soltner
Lucille Stakee
Lee Standen
Bonnie Stern
Terry Thompson
Christine Tittel
Suneeta Vaswani
Vincenzo, Washington, D.C.
Jan Weimer
Tonee Wilen
Xenios, San Francisco, California
Gilda Barrow Zimmar

Additional text was supplied by:
Cherry Hamman, *Tips and Techniques:*
    Roasting Vegetables;

The Knapp Press
is a wholly owned subsidiary of
KNAPP COMMUNICATIONS CORPORATION.

Composition by Publisher's Typography

This book is set in Sabon, a face designed by Jan Teischold in 1967 and based on early fonts
engraved by Garamond and Granjon.